I0095374

The Black Blazer

Volume I

Dr. Carl D. Wilson Jr.

HAVANA BOOK GROUP LLC
HAVANABOOKGROUP.COM

THE BLACK BLAZER

MEN ENTREPRENEURS "BLAZING TO SUCCESS"

In Dedication To

Pastor Carl D
Wilson Jr.

I dedicate this book to my father, **Pastor Carl D Wilson Jr.,** who passed away of cancer 11 years ago. He was a mentor, ROLE model, great father, and husband. WE love you dad; this book is dedicated to you.

Carl D Wilson III

I dedicate this book THE BLACK BLAZER, to my son **Carl D Wilson III;** I want this book to inspire him, to be great and a huge success in this world.

Kai Kelly

I dedicate this book to my grandson **Kai Kelly**; I want this book to inspire him. Kai has the desire to be an Author someday. These inspiring stories will motivate him to be an international bestselling author.

Preston Carl
Wilson

I dedicate this book to Preston Carl Wilson. To inspire , encourage, motivate and inspire him to be as successful.

Preston
Spikes

This book is dedicated to my brother-in-law, Preston Spikes, for always honoring and supporting the Wilson Family.

The Black Blazer Book: Volume 1

Dr. Carl D. Wilson
Author/Creator

The Black Blazer Book is an anthology of phenomenal men co-authors. These men took the time to prepare and write their chapters to inspire and encourage other men to be great and achieve their goals. The chapters are about their bios, lifestyles, goals, families, travels, and things that make them the perfect role models to support men empowerment and entrepreneurs. The goal of the first volume of *The Black Blazer* anthology is to inspire, uplift, and encourage other men to write a book or anthology to impact other men.

The Black Blazer is dedicated to Dr. Carl D. Wilson, Jr.'s son. He wants to be a positive role model for Carl D. Wilson, III. The ultimate goal is to become a best-selling author with the phenomenal co-authors of this great book. It will be a incredible accomplishment for all men involved in *The Black Blazer, Vol. 1* anthology. I want to say thank you in advance to the editor, publisher, co-authors, charitable foundation, and readers. The launch will be 28 February 2022.

Founder/CEO

+9512415343 ☎

www.cdwilsonevents.com 🌐

carldean619@gmail.com ✉

All rights reserved. No part of this publication may be reproduced, stored in a retrieval system, or transmitted in any form or by any means – electronic, mechanical, photocopying, recording or otherwise – without the written permission of the publisher.

HAVANA BOOK GROUP LLC
43537 RIDGE PARK DRIVE
TEMECULA, CA. 92590

COPYRIGHT 2021 All rights reserved.
ISBN: 978-1-73531-175-3

Endorsements

Miyoshi
Gordon, D. Hum.

I, Miyoshi Gordon, endorses the Black Blazer Men Entrepreneurs "Blazing To Success" Book. The inspirational stories are very empowering and captivating. The coauthors will have a remarkable impact on lives across nations of nations. Their transparency of story-telling is powerful in correlations of life's circumstances. Congratulations Dr. Carl D. Wilson, Jr. on your phenomenal work to continue inspiring others to "Never Give Up" on living their divine purpose in life.

Miyoshi Gordon, D. Hum.
Humanitarian, Award-Winning Author,
Advocate, Speaker

Dr Desziree
Richardson

The Black Blazer Book is an unprecedented collaboration of dynamic men who have joined forces to unlock a phenomenal chapter of wisdom, Impact and insight into their journey of self-discovery and success.

Princess Prof Dr Desziree Richardson

H.E. Dr. Rosalind
Willis

I H.E. Dr. Rosalind Willis endorses the Black Blazer Men Entrepreneurs "Blazing Toward Success" This is a book filled with Kings, Sons, Husbands, Leaders that are making a difference in our world. The stories in this book will inspire, empower, and motivate you to blaze your own path to success. Dr. Carl Wilson hand-picked some Amazing Gentlemen, and you will be blessed when you read this honorable work. Let it impact you and propel you into your own destiny.

Vanessa Jacqueline
D'cruz

I, Vanessa Jacqueline D'cruz, endorse the Black Blazer Book. The stories written in this book by the authors are empowering, intriguing and fascinating and inspiring. In our lives as we pursue to empower ourselves, this book serves as a source of great enlightenment. The authors come from various friends and this book is rich in experiences. We can learn from these great experiences. Congratulations Dr. Carl D Wilson on your exemplary choice of authors.

Queen Corazon
Ugalde Armenta

The Black Blazer Book is eloquently written by amazing and successful men of different backgrounds with impressive accomplishments!

Congratulations Dr. Carl Wilson and all the phenomenal co-authors!
by Queen Corazon Ugalde Armenta

Chapter Overview

Dr. Asgar Mahomed

Be the Change
By Dr. Asgar Mahomed

Managing Director of Esquire, Film Producer at Film Chrome

"Be the Change" has always been the driving vision for Asgar Mahomed. Asgar has been a serial entrepreneur for as long as he can remember.

From humble beginnings, two years of hitch-hiking from Pretoria to Johannesburg to study computer programming and back home, assembling computers on their mom's dining room table to listing a company on the Johannesburg Securities Exchange as Casey Investment Holdings Limited, selling it and then starting Esquire Technologies. Asgar Mahomed together with his brother Mahomed Cassim have become one of the leading South African information technology and digital lifestyle product resellers in South Africa.

For as long as Asgar can remember they have been entrepreneurs, selling diverse items such as bracelets and toys to their classmates and others during their school days.

While studying at a computer college in Johannesburg, they sold audio cassettes and floppy disks to fellow students. Doing repairs on electrical and electronic items on their mom's dining room table, their sales and part-time work earned them their starting capital which they used to assemble computers. Through sheer determination, hard work, and commitment, the brothers acquired stocks of components. They spent many evenings assembling computers, catching up with just a few hours of sleep before they headed out for deliveries. Eventually people were driving up from outlining areas as well as Durban and Cape Town to fetch their PC's. In 1989 the brothers opened their first IT shop. In 1998 they saw the Casey Group and their retail chain, Micro Matrix Computers listed on the Johannesburg Stock Exchange, making Mahomed then 31, and Asgar 30, the youngest persons to be a part of the prestigious stock exchange.

In its thirteen years of existence Casey grew immensely and was voted the sixth largest distributor in South Africa by the Corporate Research Foundation. In 1999 Casey was then sold to the Black Information Technology Empowerment Company (BLITEC).

After a well-deserved break from the industry, the brothers decided to use their entrepreneurial skills to empower smaller retailers in a rapidly growing SMME market. The idea of Esquire Technologies was born in a container with Asgar, Mahomed, and two other staff members. The company has successfully over the years grown nationally and employs over 120 staff members.

In 2004, it was announced that South Africa had won the bid to host the 2010 FIFA World Cup Soccer.

In 2007, Asgar investigated and found out that no other company ever licensed any IT or IT accessories under the FIFA brand and took it as a challenge to become the first company in the world to do so. The processes were difficult and had to be strictly conformed to FIFA's standards, which took almost a year to be perfected and finalized.

In 2009 and 2010 Asgar's company was supplying IT accessories to countries all over the world under the FIFA brand.

Asgar always had a passion for movies and this passion got him involved in the movie industry initially on marketing and branding. Asgar contacted a number of movie producers and negotiated trade off deals for IT equipment in exchange for product placement of his products and brands in a number of movies. This created such a great branding awareness for the Esquire brand in South Africa.

Thinking ahead, Asgar then set up a movie production company, Film Chrome, to become more involved in the movie industry by producing local South African movies. This became a new successful business venture and to date has produced 22 movies.

In 2009 even whilst on holiday in Durban, Asgar looked for marketing opportunities for Esquire. Asgar spotted a young talented sand sculpture artist, Zanile Nakopo, on the beachfront, who earned a living on handouts. Asgar took the opportunity to assist Zanile in guiding and empowering him in creating his own business. Asgar used his marketing talent and got Zanile to design and create a sand sculpture for "Esquire" on the beach front and remunerated Zanile.

The Durban beach has hundreds of people walking by daily and this sculpture was visible and seen by many as this was the only sand sculpture on the beach with a company logo. It became so popular, and many people passing took photos and posted it on their social media, which led to Asgar offering prizes for the best and most creative photo with the sand sculpture.

The idea became a permanent one, and Zanile was paid monthly for changing and managing the sculpture. Other companies then approached Zanile wanting a similar sand sculpture with their logos. Today Zanile is a small medium businessman and maintains monthly around 10 to 15 corporate logos on the beach. He has stopped taking handouts and has earn a fixed amount from all his clients.

Over the years Esquire Technologies has also scooped over 100 national and international awards. Asgar was awarded the FNB Islamic Finance Businessmen of the Year award in 2009 as well as nominated as a finalist for the Top Entrepreneur of the Year Award in 2010 and again in 2011 for the African Access

National Business Awards. Asgar was also nominated as a finalist in the Exceptional Category of the 2013 EY World Entrepreneur Awards. In 2014, Esquire Technologies won the Multichannel Initiative Award and was nominated as a finalist in the Innovation through Technology category in the National Business Awards in 2015, the Best Computer Hardware Company-African Corporate Excellence Awards by CV Magazine in 2016, and a finalist in the KZN Top Business Awards for 2017.

Under the umbrella of Asgar's company, Esquire has supported and donated equipment to a number of school labs and libraries.

In 2012, Esquire donated computers and sporting equipment to the Lenasia Secondary School in Johannesburg.

In July 2013, Esquire together with The Caring Women's Forum Pretoria planted vegetables and fed over 650 school children at the N' wa-mhinga Primary School in Attridgeville in Pretoria. A netball and soccer field was set up, and the sick bay was renovated.

In 2014, the Rosina Sedibane Modiba Sport School in Laudium was painted by the Esquire team, the school's computer lab was revamped, and Esquire ensured that all the computers were fully operational. Esquire's technical team also installed a fiber optic link between the schools main building and the computer lab providing full internet access to the school. Basic outdoor equipment, such as benches and tables, were also supplied for the children to enjoy their lunch during their break times or to use them for study purposes.

Esquire together with the Caring Women's Forum Pretoria as well as the Gift of the Givers hosted a "Walk for a Blanket and Eliminate Hunger". This became a yearly inaugural walk which brought in approximately 2,000 participants, spectators, and volunteers to partake in either a 5km or 7km fun walk in and around the suburbs of Laudium with the aim of raising funds for the purchasing of blankets for the needy as well as to collect canned food for the underprivileged in the Pretoria Central Business District.

In 2017, Asgar and his team at Esquire supported the Little Eden Society, an organization that provides full-time care to children and adults with profound intellectual disabilities.

Over the years, Asgar used his company and the team to support organizations, such as Crime Line, Shout SA, and Reach for a Dream Foundation and on an annual basis participates in Laudium Social Golf Club Charity Challenge to raise funds for various charity organizations, such as Sunrise School Laudium, which is a School for the Mentally Handicapped, Laudium Child Welfare, Laudium Cancer Association, and many others.

Asgar serves as the Deputy Vice President for The Minara Chamber of Commerce. This organization, which was established in 2000, works closely with all foreign embassies and provides guidance and support to a large number of their members to establish new business networks and opportunities by exposing its members to local and international trade delegations throughout South Africa.

Since 2016, Asgar has been involved with the Al-Najda Foundation, providing bursaries to students with the skills, commitment, and drive to progress their education, facing financial hurdles.

As of this date, the Al Najda Foundation has assisted over 2,000 students in bursaries allowing them to enter universities.

In 2019, Asgar was nominated to become a Global Goodwill Ambassador. Global

Humanitarian's mission is to solve real-life problems in the most disadvantaged parts of the world and to assist women, children, the hungry, and the homeless.

Asgar was nominated in the top 100 Difference in Change Makers S.A., One Billion Dreams Global Movement in September 2019. In January 2021, Asgar received a Doctorate in Humanitarian from the Global International Alliance for his contribution to the betterment of society. In February 2021, Asgar has been appointed as the Vice President for the International Youth Society for the South African Chapter.

In 2021, Asgar was awarded a special President's Volunteer Service Gold Award as well as a Lifetime Achievement Award from the President of the United States of America, President Joseph R. Biden, Jr.

As an entrepreneur from an early age with years of knowledge and experience, Asgar has always been keen on passing on his business skills and acumen by acting as a business mentor to young and upcoming entrepreneurs.

Asgar reveals the secret to his business is in purchasing products at the best pricing with great negotiating skills" as well as not overstocking products and working on the JIT system (Just in Time).

Asgar lives a balanced life by making time for his family, businesses, and sports.

THE BLACK BLAZER

MEN ENTREPRENEURS "BLAZING TO SUCCESS"

Saf Buxby

Breaking the Fantasy
of Living in a One-sided World
By Saf Buxby

Dr. Saf Buxy is a Social Behavioral Mentor and Addiction Specialist. He is an Author, Speaker, TV, Radio and Social Media personality, and respected pioneer in Addiction Consulting. He delivers life-changing material and personal expertise to shift clients towards a more fulfilling future.

Through gaining personal empirical knowledge, Dr. Saf Buxy incorporates this experience along with research, training, and vocation in guiding those afflicted by trauma and addiction. The complexity of human behavior requires a non-prescriptive approach; Saf transforms people's lives through mentally disbanding the cause of their pain.

As a proponent of breaking free from 'the madness', Saf has successfully liberated numberless individuals from tribulation so that they continue to lead a fruitful and inspiring life. His process, The Buxy Recovery Process, will liberate thousands of people from their burdens.

He is a recovered addict, an abuse victim, and above all a survivor. Saf can candidly talk about his experiences to help others liberate themselves from the attachments to any addiction- food, drugs, sex, technology, and more. His approach incorporated modalities that identify the subconscious reasons for the undesired behavior, which reveals the path to healing and brings hope for a better future.

His shows include Saf Talks, Mens Talk---a Feel Good Factor TV show on SKY Showcase 191, and a show on Spirituality Gone Wild. He also co-founded a Non-Profit, The Way Out Foundation, which has earned him the following awards:

Global Humanitarian Award
Global Change Maker (LOANI & World Leaders Association)
MENTORx
Dr Sarvepalli Radhakrishnan Award (Award of Honor)
Breakthrough International Bible University
An honorary Doctorate Degree in Humane Letters

Saf's new book, Out of the Madness: A Message of Hope has been published in March 2021. This autobiography is written to help others wake up out of their unhealthy habits to see their gifts.

If you're looking for happiness without sadness, health without disease, pleasure without pain, and more, then you're living in the lowest level of our animal brain, the amygdala; you're looking for a dopamine fix. You're being sold the fantasy that there is positive without negative. The more you strive for a one-sided world looking for the fantasy, the more your life becomes a nightmare; you're striving for something that is not available and trying to avoid something that is unavoidable. In Buddhism they used to say that desiring something that is not available and avoiding something that is not avoidable is a source of human suffering. When you live by your highest values, you embrace pleasure and pain. When you live by your highest values, you embrace support and challenge equally. But when you're living in your animal nature, you lower your values, and off you go towards a one-sided world. If you want to be a master, you must live by your highest values and wake up your executive centre that has reason and embrace both sides of life objectively, or otherwise you'll be vulnerable to the animal's behaviour, and you'll be sold the fantasy searching for the unavailable and trying to avoid the unavoidable. Anytime you get addicted to a fantasy you create a nightmare out of your life.

Anecdotal experiences are, of course, respective, yet I am a firm believer that a lesson lived is a lesson learned. Through the tumultuous of my life, I have ascertained a certain comprehension of addiction and trauma which cannot be taught or read; thus, this conceivably gives me the authority to share my experience in the hope of helping others. I currently embody the role of a recovered addict, Professional Speaker, Social Behavioural Mentor, Addiction Specialist, Radio and Talk Show Presenter, Author, Co-Founder of "Healing for the Nations" (a charity dedicated in establishing humanitarian relief initiatives globally), but above all a survivor. My mission is to give those who are suffering a message of hope and help these individuals transform their lives in a peaceful, powerful and in a way congruent to their highest priority values. There is no telos to my journey, but I simply hope that I can help people become mentally, emotionally, and physically free along the way so that they too can become survivors that have overcome and thrived in the face of adversity. I find that it helps enormously to talk about my trauma, mental health and addiction, and subsequent recovery; my philosophy is that if I can spare even one person from going down the path I did, then everything I do will be worth it. I am by no means asserting that I am an omnipotent being that can transform the indomitable, but I hope to act as a mentor and ally because I am someone who understands how to rebuild a life even if there is seemingly no way back.

Addiction does not discriminate. Many people have the preconceived impression of an addict to be an unaspiring and apathetic person, maybe someone with pitiable hygiene whose life solely revolves around their addiction. Whilst I can subscribe to the thought that an addiction is debilitating and at times all-consuming, the stereotype of what an addict is should be dispelled. I was born into a very dysfunctional family but was adopted at birth by a wonderful middle-class family, attended an acclaimed boarding school, and grew up to be a loving husband and father. Despite my ostensibly picture-perfect life, I became ensnared by the power of addiction which caused havoc in my life and affected my loved ones to a great degree.

I am yet to determine if I was born an addict or if it is a consequence of some of the woes that life threw at me. But what I do know is that addiction is not the problem but the solution to the problem or as we say in conscious recovery-a brilliant strategy. I was abused physically, racially, verbally, and sexually for six years of my life on a daily basis from the age of eleven. I suffered wounding bereavements and developed an inferiority complex which can be affiliated to my circle of friends, family members, and adoption. I was diagnosed as bipolar. To be frank, I don't know if these events caused my addiction or if it was some sort of predisposition, but I do know that I am an addict and will always be an addict. It may sound counter-intuitive to some that I use the term addict in the present tense when my aim is to help people change their lives, but for me it all comes down to accepting the addiction. Acceptance is the answer to all my problems today. It was unnerving for me to ask for help, but in all honesty, it was scarier to continue to do what I was doing. My destructive behaviour and volatile mental health that addiction caused plagued my life to becoming unmanageable, but a person may have to hit rock-bottom to value his existence. I vehemently believe that the potency of my self-destruction led me to recovery.

I find it difficult to verbalize the extent of the perils of addiction or the 'madness' as I call it---primarily because addiction often causes a loss of inhibition and rational thought; I used to act uncharacteristically, sometimes delving into the realm of the unethical. In retrospect, coming from a place of recovery, my past self is unrecognizable and the way that I acted seems so senseless as I am now enlightened to the splendour of sobriety. The most tangible effects of addiction are seen in the pain of my loved ones. During the madness, I both financially and emotionally bankrupted my family. It's not like that today. Through my work, whether it be private consultations, workshops, or platforms, I help people become empowered self-leaders who choose to self-govern. My work which I serve globally stems from a metacognitive perspective and the application of omnipresent laws. These Laws regulate with precision all aspects of creation---all events, conditions, and circumstances experienced by everyone personally and collectively. I believe once you understand, apply, and align yourself with Universal Laws, you will experience transformation in every area of your life and in turn live a fulfilling prosperous life.

- There is a universal intelligence that exceeds human understanding.

- All humans have an innate desire to learn, grow, and achieve their soulful purpose.

- Everything is impermanent, ever-changing, and transforming.

- When we unite our minds and hearts together, we create synergy.

- Our adaptability to challenges is key to our evolution as beings.

- Each of us is contributing to the development of our species.

- The individual with the most flexible thinking has the most self-governance.

In 1983, I had my first drink, a bottle of vodka neat. I was eleven years old. Subsequently, I was unconscious for over nine hours and had my first of two stomach pumps. This was the start of a 33-year addiction---an addiction that has caused pain, destruction, chaos, and a lot of mayhem.

Through my personal and professional experience in addiction, I've been looking at myself and some of the addicts in my life with whom I work and have been trying to work out how I can be of service and help in some way to them and in my growth. I realized there were loads of incredibly basic questions to which I just didn't know the answer, such as what really causes addiction? Why do we carry on with this approach that doesn't seem to be working? Is there a better way out there that we could try instead? I read loads of journals about it, studied, and researched daily in recovery. I engaged myself in the works of Dr John Demartini, Dr Gabor Mate, TJ Woodward, Bruce Alexander, Professor Marcantonio Spada, and Dr Viktor Frankl to see if I could learn from these incredible specialists in their respective fields. I ended up working in the field of addiction and human behaviour. The thing I realized that became apparent is almost everything I thought I knew about addiction was wrong.

What is "The Buxy Recovery Process"? Well, what if underneath all addictive behaviour is an essential self that is whole and perfect. This what I'm experiencing now. I feel like the luckiest person alive, so open, so present, and so deeply connected with my essential truth, the love that I am, and that I was.

Being around people throughout my life especially when I was a vulnerable eleven-year-old, being told that I looked like a fat brown Terrorist, being told I was ugly, and being told I was thick, etc., etc., I quickly realized based on the energy that that was not okay. Those experiences along with thousands that I could name created not only this wall but a belief in my own brokenness. So I walked around from age eleven, feeling disconnected, feeling broken, and feeling as if there was something fundamentally wrong with me and with the world. Soon after, I found relief from that. It came in the form of drugs and alcohol. As a matter of fact, the moment I drank that bottle of vodka for the first time, I felt alive again.

It brought relief from that psychic pain that I was in; it brought relief for me carrying around these core beliefs of my own unworthiness. I have come to recognize that drugs and alcohol are not the problem. They're actually a solution. In my own life, they were a solution to my belief in my own brokenness. Now, I'm not just talking about a belief in my mind I had cemented, the energy of brokenness, that I am not lovable, I'm not good enough, I am not worthy. I carried these core false beliefs around for many years. I found relief from alcohol and drugs. So by the time I turned 43, I did come into recovery. That began my journey of returning to the essential truth of who and what I am. "The Buxy Recovery Process" focuses primarily on the emotional and spiritual components coupled with your highest priority values and omnipresent laws in particular The Law of Duality. "The Buxy Recovery Process" works with a set of questions and tools to help you become self- empowered leaders.

My story is by no means idyllic, but the falling action is nothing short of a dream. The anguish of my loved ones propelled my rehabilitation and sobriety. In the past, there were many transient attempts of being sober, but these were short-lived as I was in constant denial that I was an addict. In these instances, I never effusively sought help and merely replaced one addiction with another which continued to fuel my dependence on the external. However, this time it was different; I started working the well-known twelve step program. Like many I was apprehensive that this would work; the program is often sardonically depicted in film and tv: 'My name is Saf, and I am an addict'. But shortly after starting, I appreciated that it was more than just a recovery program but a program of life. I can submit to the fact that the twelve steps are not for everyone, but many elements are germane to anyone wanting to relieve their lives of addiction and compulsive behaviours. Principally, it enabled my understanding of what it is to be immobilized against my addiction and that sobriety required constant introspection and contemplation to work. In the ensuing time, I engaged in further outpatient rehab and became an avid attendee of various support groups. Arguably, for the first time in my life, I didn't feel alone. I'm not undermining the love and support of my family, but I am resolute in the idea that only a fellow addict can fully comprehend the inner turmoil faced on a day-to-day basis. The support groups encouraged a sense of solidarity; everyone had the same goal, and this safe space created a camaraderie that is ineffable. Aspire2Be Recovery was another group that helped the transformation of my life; ironically, I am now a trustee of this community, evident that life really can come full circle.

A fundamental aspect of my journey was therapy. I was treated by a remarkable therapist who allowed me to dispatch my trauma, and we spoke in depth about my adolescence. We talked openly about the gravity of my past disburdened my mind, which allowed me to propel into recovery without a heaviness weighing me down. Self-examination is so vital in obstructing the power of addiction. How can you stop what consumes your mind when you do not understand your mind?

Through diligently improving myself personally, the only logical progression was to help others who were not exposed to such wonderful services. Subsequently, I committed to volunteering in the drug and alcohol services and moved beyond the empirical and started to study various schools of thought. I worked as a practitioner at a 'lifers' prison which was an eye-opening experience to say the least. As bizarre as it may sound, I have always relished in surrounding myself around criminals, perhaps you could say I felt at home. Many of the inmates that I encountered mirrored my disposition; they often experienced abuse in the past, but it was evident that the crimes they committed were intrinsically uncharacteristic. Substance abuse can give you a deceitful sense of control, which they may have lacked in their life, and can provide a feigned confidence. I felt it was vital to be of aid in the rehabilitation process even for criminals who had committed the most ghastly crimes. To limit the number of reoffenders and enlighten people to choose an enhanced life path was my ultimate ambition.

The aforementioned aspiration that I learnt from my voluntary work has transcended into present day. Through my own brand "Saf's Surgery", I work as a Radio and Sky TV host and professional speaker on shows/topics dedicated to addiction, trauma, and mental Health. I'm a Social Behavioral Coach trained in Metacognitive Therapy, The Demartini Method and Conscious Recovery, where I see clients individually and/or in groups by the way of facilitating workshops and presenting my own creation "The Buxy Recovery Process", and I intend to dedicate the rest of my life helping people by giving a message of hope.

Author of "Out of The Madness: A Message of Hope"
Saf Buxy
www.safbuxy.com
info@safbuxy.com

Dr. Saf Buxy
www.safbuxy.com

Coach MJ Tolan

Serendipity
By Coach MJ Tolan

They say that serendipity is when you are looking for something but then stumble across something even more wonderful along the journey.

I am not sure how any of my story happened, but it feels like a combination of Forrest Gump meets Frodo. I was the first born of eight boys to Irish Catholic parents in Columbia. I always enjoyed how this sounded to people overseas who must have scanned me again head to toe upon hearing that and looked for any South American physical traits.

Nope.

This was Columbia, South Carolina.

Having seven brothers and being the eldest meant that I would carry the enormous and perpetual responsibility of setting the example for my younger brothers. Oh well.

Remember summers?

My mother would quickly realize that idle boys, especially during school breaks, would be up to pure mischief. Well, she was right, of course. How could we not want to explore the woods and ride bikes in the moonlight? So, even before we were shepherded off to summer jobs, our household and yard chores were publicly posted on an appliance where there could be no denial that we had not seen it… the refrigerator door.

Genius.

On Mondays MJ would have dish duties, Patrick would have laundry, Timothy would have table clearing duty, and Shawn did the yard raking. The list was revised every week. In a very short period of time, it became obvious that the elder brothers could pass their duties onto their younger brothers for completion. It felt like exploitation of opportunity at first until later in life I learned that this art was actually taught in Harvard University.

They called it 'Executive Delegation'.

Marvelous.

I remember the first time that I, like the character Frodo in Lord of the Rings, recognized that I had gone further from home than ever before, and it was actually a bit exhilarating and yet frightening. It was a self-navigated journey on the other side of the town I was born in, but nevertheless, I felt like a real explorer, perhaps even a bit like Marco Polo that we had been told about in school, where I spent most of my time daydreaming.

School I had decided was not for me. I did not feel as if I fit in and was not academically interested. By my 17th birthday I found myself at a crossroads. Life has a way sometimes of choosing you... young boys a bit older than me had been drafted to go to war. I enrolled in the military as a Combat Medic. I had been inspired by the fun-loving zany cast of a movie and later a TV series that followed called M.A.S.H. about a bunch of crazy fun-loving medical teams in a field hospital during war time.

A real war was happening in Asia. I was told "they" needed me, and so I rose to the call--all 125 pounds of my skinniness. When I was told I had been selected to go to Vietnam after bootcamp, I was totally elated as I had been promised during my training that this is where I would learn the most as a field medic.

To my dismay, I later learned, due to my most fortunate timing, the war had come to an abrupt halt. My orders were cancelled, and I was reassigned to a different lifestyle destination.

Alaska.

Our mission, we were told, was to guard the Bering Straits from our enemy known to us as the Communist Russians. 'The Soviets' were only 60 miles across the frozen sea. Lucky for me I was assigned to an infantry unit, so we were able to practice marching in the snow at 40 degrees below zero for hours and hours. In the evenings we would have fun sleeping in frozen tents in the same snow-covered woods.

It was cold there, like all the time. I saw grown men cry, and then I watched their tears turn to Ice as if in some sci-fi movie had released a freeze weapon. Oh, and it was dark, too, like I mean all the time. In December the sun would barely open its eyes and then close again, like some kind of teasing wink, so we are talking twenty hours of darkness.

I made a personal promise to myself to move to the tropics as soon as I got out of this Ice Prison.

What an inspiration.

As soon as I was a civilian again, I moved to Myrtle Beach, South Carolina. Here was the sun, the beach, young people having fun, and a satellite campus of the University of South Carolina.

I enrolled as a freshman, got two part time jobs to pay my rent, and was off to the races. I became a proud academic. I ran for class president and won. I had a 4.0 GPA. I had never had any grades like these in my life! I had landed in heaven. I discovered that I could do well in school, do well in my jobs, and I had decided leapfrog from medic to medical degree.

Then, while having breakfast in a tourist Waffle House, everything changed. A man approached me who had seen me talking to several people in the restaurant and offered me a job in sales, citing he liked my bubbly personality.

Well, how about that?

He challenged me for thirty days saying if I use all my skills, I would never want to change my job after a month.

Game on.

Within ten days I had earned more money in commissions than my favorite university professor did in a month. The business was called timeshare, and I was hooked. I stayed late and listened to the more experienced sales champions finish up their meetings with clients every night for months learning as if I were an insatiable sponge. I also cross educated myself on lead generation and marketing methods.

I was promoted to go to a new site in Florida; hello Frodo, here we go again.

The tropics.

Within a year I had a stunning title, shining sports car, and an ego larger than a school bus. I had spent a weekend in Miami in the B-Gees' studio after attending my buddy's birthday party arriving by private plane. I had yet to celebrate my 23rd birthday so I was in my mind… a very cool guy. Like I said, I had an ego the size of a bus, a double decker.

I started my own business at age 24, and more and more of my younger brothers began to visit and do on-the-job-training. We were going up and up. From Orlando to London, I led start -up operations for sales and marketing teams. I was fortunate to be hard working, always reading and listening to positive mental attitude tapes to sharpen my own thinking.

From having projects off the coast of Africa to the Greek islands, my life was unrecognizable to that young man who had felt an empty hole in his belly the first time he was six miles from home.

During all my travels and exploits as fate would have it, boy meets girl. She was lovely, from Lebanon, enchanting, French speaking. I had no chance of fending this one off. She had met me in one of my career dips, the roller coaster that I have been riding for years with the ups and downs of business success. Oh yes, sometimes there were empty days and empty pockets. So I knew she was not in it for the money.

But I had friends, and these friends would never abandon me either …They were my mentors, the authors whose stories sustained me, motivated me, stirred my imagination, and challenged me.

Zig Ziglar, Brian Tracy, Dr, Robert Schuler, Napoleon Hill, W. Clemens Stone, Vince Lombardi, Gene Rodenberry, and others were my personal motivational coaches I had adopted.

After a few short years together with my newfound love, I was in a burn your boats moment. The iron curtain had fallen; literally, this was the collapse of the Soviet Union. New countries emerged as free nations and new open borders. There was a blue ocean of new markets to be explored full of opportunity.

What was Frodo to do?

I could not sleep for months, pacing and studying any financial data and research I could find, pre-internet on the eastern block of countries. With no data available, I was forced to visit the countries for fact finding trips. Finally, I selected a country by lifestyle wealth. This was done by looking out of the window of the taxi from the airport and checking the quality of new cars and TV satellite dishes on the roofs of homes and apartment blocks. I saw evidence-based science in action.

Maybe I had actually learned something in school. That was my market study in a nutshell. Thank you! So now that had all the facts I could muster, should I remain where I was or jump?

Do I stay where I am and remain safe and comfortable or risk it all and go for it with no parachute?

The plan was simple. Surrender any and all income to be able to move to a new country where you know absolutely not one single person, do not speak the language or understand the laws, and risk all your savings.

Now, who could turn down such an amazingly tempting proposal?

I remembered from history that pioneers end up with arrows in their backs.

No problem, right?

BOOOOM!

I opened my first company two weeks before we married and never looked back. Within two years we had established offices in four countries with 300 staff. After four years, we were thinking of divesting and retirement.

I did.

For about six weeks. We then started a new company inside Lebanon.

What could possibly go wrong?

That is a whole other story... but let's keep this one going ... Upon moving to my wife's homeland in Beirut, I had a major wakeup call...This was when it became evident that my French speaking charming spouse was actually the daughter of some very Arabic parents. I should have known there might be a culture clash when playing rock music at our wedding raised eyebrows ... and judgment. I had never felt so much like a foreigner in my life.

Fast forward two years and I was the topic of every three-hour lunch; yes, Lebanese can sit, eat, talk, and eat for three hours straight on a Sunday. I found myself in a conversation in Arabic, barely catching one out of fifty words, and then, like gears on a motorcycle, they would effortlessly switch to French for ten minutes, English for ten seconds, and back to Arabic.

My wife's parents were getting along in age (both in their 70's) and the hints about "Where are the grandkids" were now deafening. The problem was that my wife had already been pregnant on four different occasions only to have the empty disappointment and loss each time. Losing a child after three to four months of pregnancy is a devastating loss and this was taking a toll on her and our relationship. So they blamed me, the foreigner. It must be him… is what I imagined they were saying over tabouli salad.

Meanwhile, doctors were consulted in every corner of the planet for another two years but with no result. She became more desperate to become a mom, and I simply did not want to see her continue to be disappointed. I just knew adoption would be the next step. I felt so bad for her the fifth time she found out she was pregnant that I bought her a puppy; yes, don't judge. I was hoping she would have some emotional support before I traveled again to go open a new country office when the inevitable predictable loss happened.

And then, Magic.

We found out that she was going to deliver this time as she had carried beyond the danger zone. The Ultrasound revealed we would be blessed with twins.

Blessings be upon us.

I decided right then and there to give thanks by starting a movement for less fortunate children who had no parents ever to spend an hour with them playing or reading to them. Afterall, we were heading toward adoption anyway. I assembled my team overseas for a brainstorming session, and we planned our first Tolan Family funded event for less fortunate kids.

How to marry what we do for a living with our new passion to empower kids …

Eureka!!!

I named our movement Time 4 Sharing to celebrate that spending time with kids that mattered was an awesome privilege and gift while tying it to our professional business. By now we had purchased travel agencies, started our own timeshare vacation club, and had marketing franchises operating our sales in multiple markets.

We knew that this was a mission of goodwill; we could not find parents for these kids or cure diseases, but our formula was going to be spending quality time with kids that mattered. Anytime anyone does something that seems noble or pure at heart, it attracts a group of naysayers who are right there, sneering, snickering, judging, and condescending.

I did not want to give these little people a chance, so I created a Manta, Our Mission is to 'Raise Fun, Not Funds, for Kids that Matter'.

I would fund everything myself.

We met with a local zoo in Prague and agreed to sponsor and name an animal in their habitat. I chose a Kangaroo and named her Boomerang. Mother Kangaroos have a pouch where babies can ride a long, how cool is that. So, our first event was planned one day before the twins were born.

The Czech Republic has one of the most beautiful capital cities in the world, and the zoo is exceptional. We had found an orphanage to invite thirty kids and created a ceremony to make them all Moms and Dads of our new mascot, Boomerang. The children adopted the Kangaroo!

On the 13th of November, thirty smiling children connected

with a kangaroo as few had ever done, 24 hours before the expected birth of our own twins. All my volunteers were our staff members, and they were electrified with the experience of seeing how happy these kids really were. I jumped on a plane that night thinking I had just experienced the greatest most satisfying day of my life.

The next morning, I witnessed the birth of our twins, best day ever... This seemed to motivate me even more to expand the vision of our charity work. This movement grew from one event to seven events within a year, and there was no end in sight. Events were held in Bahrain, Lebanon, Czech Republic, and Slovakia.

We became an officially registered NGO, Non-Profit Charity and since our beginnings have had over 10,000 Children participate in our programs.

We began to realize that this movement had taken on a life of its own. We discovered that we could organize 'Edu-tainment' events for kids that had social and community impact. We were able to attract 'heads of state', celebrities, and other notables, such as Olympic medal winners, musicians, and sports stars in the countries where we had offices. We also teamed up with Special Olympics, Red Cross, and so many other charities to joint venture events, always showcasing our Boomerang mascot and teaching the kids to sing a universal chant that I had invented: "Osta – Bosta – Boosta"!!! It was explained to them by our local translators that kangaroos respond to these words and bring candy and sweets! So imagine children who only understand Arabic or Croatian, Slovakian, Czechian, all uniting under this song, this movement. Osta – Bosta – Boosta!

Sometimes there were more than 400 children in one single event so just imagine the enthusiastic chanting! We were so hooked. We created story books for the environment and appointed an animator to produce our own coloring books which we handed out in schools. We chanted our anthem by shouting: Osta- Bosta – Boosta!

Our events included The Million Words of Hope Book Drives, United Hearts of Lebanon, Running for Smiles and Smiles Marathon, The Lights of Lebanon and more. We were outdoing ourselves event after event. The momentum was incredible.

We even joined forces with The United Nations special envoy in southern Lebanon who had been removing land mines and agreed to plant trees along the border of Israel. This idea was born during a photo opportunity standing in front of a statue we had created for the United Nations Palace in Beirut standing and speaking with The First Lady of Lebanon and the UN Special Envoy.

We arrived there one day with our 300 volunteers in a convoy of eight school buses and planted 3000 carob – trees and built a children's park all in a single day.

What a day!

Osta – Bosta – Boosta!

My children's names were on a commemorative plaque that dedicated the trees and the playground we built.

How cool is that?

Other events we created were variations of social action and arts programs, theatre and entertainment shows, all for kids that matter.

We never accepted or solicited funds for any of our projects.

During these events we attracted notable guests, such as a real princess from Bahrain, the First Lady of Czech Republic, the President and First lady of Slovakia, The Prime Minister of Slovakia, The President and First Lady of Lebanon, and Dr.

Timothy Shriver of Special Olympics from the Kennedy family.

Our business and our charity work seemed to be all connected, and in fact, one friend told me that I was running a business part time and a full-time charity. We were having fun, more than fun; we were inspired and being guided as if this was a higher calling.

Once I had divested my business interests again, I began to follow my passion to interact with teams of people for training, speaking, and workshop events. Professionally I transitioned from CEO of fifteen years to coach and devoted my professional time to training other companies, mentor startups and businesses which is where I earned the mantle of Coach MJ

Empowering others has been and still is my lifelong passion.

I look forward to being the co-author of the next chapters in my story.

 I give all the credit to my Creator and remain in His hands. After living overseas more than thirty years, I have recently returned to my homeland in the USA.

Back ... in the Shire.

These are lessons learned from all these experiences in which we organized over 120 events for over 16,500 children:

1. You don't need money to give to kids in need; time and care is more precious.

2. One of the most motivating team building days we ever created was one of our many Time4sharing events. Our team members felt so empowered that they had been involved in something bigger, higher, and more meaningful than their normal workday because they were giving in service.

3. Giving to others is in many ways giving to yourself more than you could ever realize.

4. Although we never ever went out of our way to meet any of the notables that we did in our journey, they came, drawn to the momentum of what I called our 'processionary effect', impacting communities where we lived and worked. We created a goodwill magnetic footprint.

5. You never know what might happen when you 'Dare to leave the Shire...

During the time since I originally left on my life's journey, I have rung the success bell more than twice in business, lost it all, back and forth, lived in eight countries, started over a dozen companies... but nothing tops the giving of heart and spirit to others ...

On November 14, 2021, our twins and our charity turned 21 years old... But our work is not done... We need more united hearts to join us and volunteer to raise awareness...

Unfortunately, at the time of this writing, Lebanon is experiencing horrific poverty and hardships due to collapse of the economy, failure of the electrical supply, fuel shortages, political turmoil, and potentially religious persecution.

Time4Sharing.org has a continuous mission to empower less fortunate children with education and laughter. We remain open to new cooperation, new leadership, new initiatives, new volunteer drives no matter what.

Given the situation now is this Impossible?

Anything can be done when good people pull together: 'Osta – Bosta – Booosta'

This is why throughout my career, I have always been inspired by those who have faced down adversity and overcame the impossible.

Anyone can say something is impossible, but the possibilities are within each of us, this is why I am on this mission to inspire others, Mission: I'M Possible.

Connect with my Youtube show:

The Real Mission: I'M Possible Show with Coach MJ

Follow my podcast and connect with me on LinkedIn.

Connect with us: Together@Time4sharing.org

#tolanbrothers #Coachmjtolan #Time4sharing

@CoachMJTolan

Kenrick McDonald

When The Magical Cards Is Stacked Against You, Deal Them Anyway

By Kenrick McDonald

"Good is great when great is not present, but when greatness comes, good is only good". Kenrick McDonald

As an international award-winning entertainer/master magician, my goal is to inspire through performance, documentaries, and speaking engagements, letting the masses know that they can overcome the noise of failure. I believe that God sets our destiny, and we must identify and move toward it.

I know there are certain grammatical rules when writing; there are many clever lines, clever sayings, and soliloquies that people use to illustrate their point. Here's a popular one. I was born with a silver spoon in my mouth. Unfortunately I could never get behind that saying because the spoon that I was born with was "rusty". In fact, the cards of my journey literally were stacked against me.

As you read my words, please allow me to speak to you as if we are having a one- on-one conversation. My journey is orthodox and defies many rules. In sharing my story, I realize that life is more like a movie, and the moments in time are like snapshots of scenes in that movie. Allow me to share with you where I am now and then highlight a few snapshots of my journey. Hopefully in the future you will be able to witness the entire movie.

Allow me to introduce myself. I am Master Magician Kenrick Ice McDonald. My performances have earned me a reputation of excellence and integrity as well as the nick name "The Magical Phenomenon". I have sold out performances and broken audience and box office records around the globe. My story has been featured on several top-rated programs and documentaries including NPR with host Steve Inskeep, Masters of Illusion, The Daily Show and The Tonight Show, just to name a few. I've been featured in articles in the New York Times, The Wall Street Journal, Los Angeles Times, and many other publications and have graced the cover of at least thirteen national and international magic magazines and publications.

February 2020, I was listed as one of the Most-Influential Magicians of the Decade. One of my greatest honors was on Sunday, July 22, 2018. I was unanimously voted into The Society of American Magicians' National Magic Hall of Fame, joining a very exclusive list of magicians.

In the summer of 2014, I was inaugurated as National President of The Society of American Magicians (S.A.M.), becoming the first African American to hold this position in the 119-year history of the organization. It was a history making event. Founded in 1902, S.A.M. is the oldest and most prestigious magic organization in the world.

I'm grateful to be the recipient of many honors and awards, such as two-time "Entertainer of the Year", three Presidential Citations from national and international magic organizations, and the Commander Performer's "Medal for Excellence" presented by Commander Trent R. Pickering, U.S. Armed Services. Also I was honored by the Minister of India with the "Performer's Trophy of Honor". I was the only United States representative in the Festival of Global Magic, held in Kerala, India. I have received a "Doctorate in the Art of Magic" (a performance-based degree).

Being a sought-after lecturer, inspirational speaker, and media entertainment consultant, I have crafted several inspirational and educational programs and have authored a book entitled: "BORN FOR THIS – Destiny Authenticated".

I have produced and directed several films and documentaries.

My most recent project is an award-winning documentary entitled "Quiet Masters – The History and Relevance of the Black Magical Artist". This documentary covers some of the early and contemporary African American magicians.

The gift and my not so secret weapon

I've been asked what's your secret to your success, training, etc. Although this conversation should go deeper, I will briefly say this. The talents that I have are God given gifts... no mentors, no trainers. It goes back to my childhood, being able to figure out difficult things without instructions. I believe that my life has been touched by God. By His grace and favor, He has given me the ability to achieve at a high level. I am a Christian, and I believe that Jesus Christ is my Lord and Savior. I do believe everyone should have a belief system in his/her life to stand on ... because my friend, you will fail several times at success, no matter what level that you operate on. You will need something to lean on that encouraged you to keep moving when stopping is not the right decision and to stop when moving is detrimental to your journey.

The journey

Let's look at a few snapshots of my journey to give you some insights regarding my success.

SNAPSHOT: My magical appearance on the earth was Wednesday, July 6, 1960, at 1:46 a.m. On your mark, get set, BORN. Yes, my journey got off to a running start, and it seems as if I've been running ever since. Born in Albuquerque, New Mexico, and raised in San Diego, California. My young life was filled with many typical things that would be a part of any kid's life, but there were also events that took place that could have derailed my destiny.

SNAPSHOT: Imagine a few young kids playing in the yard and news of a serial killer killing children just hit the airways. An old car flies down the street and stops about ten feet in front of us kids. A man says in an intense voice COME HERE. I, being a naïve kid approximately six years old, began walking toward the car. My older brother grabbed my collar and shouted NO. The man's voice got violent and began to shout, "I SAID COME HERE". He drove off once we yelled for our parents. From that moment, I withdrew and became untrusting. My world became my brother, my imaginary friend "Jerome", and me.

Being a young kid that was almost kidnapped was hard to shake. In my mind everyone wanted to kidnap me, so I kept to myself, and that's when my creativity and imagination started moving toward my destiny. My imaginary friend and I began building things from twigs and old cans. To take it a step further, I started performing for an invisible audience. My mother's recollection of those times was she would hear noise coming from my room. She said that I was acting as the performer and then would jump on the other side of the room and pretend to be the audience and applaud the performance. As I look back at those times, I realize that was the genesis of who I am today.

A short time after that, I believe God endorsed my journey, and that my existence was not a mistake. My Achilles heel throughout my life has been my stomach, which was definitely the case as a young kid.

SNAPSHOT: It had been a year since my stomach began cramping, even to the point where the doctor did an exploratory surgery but did not find the issue. I was approximately seven years old, and my stomach had swollen to the size of a basketball. After several test and several X-rays, nothing was found. The medical team began preparing my mother for my death. As my mother stared down at her young son turning gray, she prayed, and in between prayers she begged the doctor to do one last X-ray. As the X-ray technician was positioning me for the final X-ray, he dropped my body on the table. That drop shifted my inside organs, causing the hidden medical issue to be revealed. Destiny almost died that day.

Fast-forward a few years to the age of nine and ten. These years did a lot to shape who I am today.

SNAPSHOT: By this time my creativity was off the charts, and Jerome my imaginary friend was still around. During that school year, I realized that I read differently than the other kids. Later to find out that I was dyslexic...I realized it at 9ish, but it was confirmed 44 years later. How ironic that I am dyslexic and having to read everything three times, I was able to author a book entitled: Born for This - Destiny Authenticated.

As a kid, things were pretty rough; my family couldn't afford much; my school clothes consisted of a couple of pairs of jeans and shirts. I had two pairs of shoes, one for church and one for school... sometimes it would be one pair. I would either have to wear church shoes to school or school shoes to church.

That same school year, my mother was in a grocery store named "Food Basket". While in that store, there was a basket filled with knock off brand tennis shoes. These were very cheap shoes, and the mates were held together by a string. They looked similar to the Chuck Taylor's Converse basketball tennis shoes.

Chuck Taylor's Converse were the desired tennis shoes of the day, the Jordan's of the era. All the kids wanted them, but only a few families could afford them, and I was not in that group. I wanted those shoes badly but could only afford the seven-dollar shoes from the grocery store. So, being creative and with the ability to draw and paint, I decided to draw the Converse logo onto the cheap tennis shoe with watercolors. Desperate to show the other kids that I could afford the high-priced shoes, I wore the altered shoes to school the next day. Unfortunately, I hadn't listened to the weather forecast. It rained, and the paint on the shoes started running, and the logo smeared; yes, I got teased.

Approximately one year after my shoe failure, someone gave the church/my father some items. Did I mention that my father was a minister, and on occasion people would give the church clothes and toys? Sometimes my brother and I would be the recipients of those things.

This particular day my father gave me some of those items, one being a second hand magic kit. Excited to get anything other than socks and underwear, I ran to open the magic kit only to find out that the kit had pieces missing. I was still able to figure out how things worked; that's when I as the magician was CONCEIVED. With my home being a strong no nonsense Christian home, there was NO encouragement for anything that didn't have to do with church, but none was needed. The problem I had was that the only successful magicians that I was exposed to were white magicians. That dilemma only lasted a short time. While watching television, I saw one of the most beautiful things I had ever witnessed up until that point, a black couple on television performing magic. It was that very moment when I as the magician was BORN because sometimes you must see the thing in order to be the thing.

SNAPSHOT: High school is the place where you change the most, and that was exactly what happened in my case. My appearance changed to the point where I gave a fellow student a ride to a modeling agency, and instead of being interested in that student, the agency asked me to become a model, and just like that my modeling career started. So now I am a student athlete, model, and an aspiring entertainer with a learning disability.

A forced change of plans will happen throughout all levels of life. That definitely was the case in my high school and college years.

As a high school student athlete, I was getting close to the end of my high school track and field career, and no major colleges were recruiting me. A local junior college coach offered me an opportunity to run for his track and field program. I accepted the coach's offer to run for the college.

A Basket Weaving Fool.

SNAPSHOT: Relinquishing your plans to someone else can derail your destiny...The first year of college, my track coach registered me for all easy classes, including four Physical Education classes and a Basket Weaving class. My circumstances had me in junior college with a coach that was only interested in my talent as a track star. Although I loved track and field, it wasn't my future aspirations, so I decided NOT to be a statistic and changed my classes to the required subjects. I then came up with a plan to show the track world the talent of my high jumping skills, so coaches would flock to offer me a scholarship.

My plans were just about to be fulfilled when a coach from San Diego State University saw me at a Championship Preliminary track meet. He was impressed by my high jumping ability. He met with my coach, and they planned to discuss the possibility of a scholarship to high jump for the university. I remember thinking "My plan is working" UNTIL...later that same day while returning from that track meet, I was attacked by two Doberman Pincher dogs. One of the dogs bit my upper thigh, tearing a plug out of it. THAT ONE INCIDENT CHANGED EVERYTHING. After the attack, I continued to model and practice magic, but my spirit was broken, and no longer being able to jump, the scholarship went away. That's when I became a professional magician.

SNAPSHOT: Jump forward a few years. Being professional does not automatically bring you success. With obligations, and that one important thing, eating, I found employment as a Department of Defense nonmilitary personnel. During my four years punching the clock, my spirit would not rest. The things that were a part of my destiny wouldn't release me; they kept yelling, THIS IS NOT IT. So imagine this, I worked eight hours during the day, performed at night, and modeled in between. While buying my time, I saw and heard all of the discouraging things one can endure. My immediate supervisor called me crazy for thinking that I could be successful in entertainment.

On this job, I saw young men my age, looking like old men. One day while working, an old grumpy white guy asked me if I was aware that I had a lazy S ... you slur your S's; I remember being devastated. All this time no one had ever told me this, not even family. I recorded myself speaking upon rewinding the tape and listening. I sat there with my mouth open thinking what am I going to do now. On top of everything, I have a speech impediment. The "NOISE" of discouragement was louder than ever. The day my destiny yelled louder than discouragement was while at work. I heard a loud commotion in the other room. A man had literally worked himself to death. The noise went silent, and for a moment I thought "That could have been me". Throughout my time there, an older man everyone called Big Ed recognized that I was different and didn't belong there. He called everyone "baby". He would always say to me "Baby - it's time to go". After my fellow employee died, a very serious Big Ed looked me directly in the eyes and said in a voice I didn't recognize, "BABY - IT'S TIME TO GO, His term of endearment "BABY" was not endearing; it was in an authoritarian voice. Shortly after that, I quit that job and relocated from San Diego to Los Angeles to pursue my dream.

Dreams can transition into nightmares if you don't diligently pursue those dreams. Upon arriving in Los Angeles, the failures kept piling up. Becoming a magical success story in L.A. was taking longer than anticipated. I had to rely on my one true positive, my looks. Modeling kept me out there, and winning the

1986 Mr. Black Los Angeles, Model of the Year Competition by combining runway modeling with magic gave me a boost in both genres. Working consistently in both industries, I believed fully to succeed I needed to make a decision, Modeling or Magic. The career lifespan of a model is a few years, and me approaching old age as a model, I chose magic. Judging how I look today, I can appreciate that decision.

In a recent conversation I was asked: did I always know that I would reach this level of success? As a young kid I knew that I would entertain or be in front of an audience.

A little known fact is that I am a big nerd, and I wonder every day when will people realize that I am a nerd in disguise.

As you read in the previous section, I am a master magician and have been performing professionally for forty years as well as being a lecturer/speaker and filmmaker. The journey for the magic is pretty clear. Regarding lecturing and speaking, I began lecturing to magicians in 1993 (28 years ago). In the magic business, there are many magic conventions and local magic clubs. Once you reach a certain status, just like other businesses, you are brought in to teach on the art. You become a magician's magician. Lecturing at these events led to speaking to corporations as well as organizations outside the magic industry. Two of my biggest confidence builders was when a Corporate CEO, after seeing my magic lecture, asked me to come to his company and give the same inspirational talk, minus the teaching of tricks, of course. He was intrigued about how one can command the stage and keep the attention of thousands. He wanted me to share that secret to his people who gave presentations.

The other confidence builder was an incident that caught me off guard. I had just finished a lecture and was standing outside the lecture hall greeting the attendees when a man approached me in silence. At the time I was engaged with another person, this guy worked his way to my side and without saying a word put an envelope in my hand and walked away. I stopped my conversation for a second to get him to return; I was unsuccessful. He disappeared around the corner. Not knowing what it was, I put the envelope in my pocket to open later. Exhausted from the lecture, upon entering my hotel room, I removed everything from my pocket and fell asleep. The next morning, I opened the envelope which contained a letter. On a side note, I always wondered if my message is being received in the manner in which I intended... The letter was from a guy named Frank, a magic enthusiast and a NASA scientist. The letter was powerful. One section stated, and I quote.

"The tools that you spoke of tonight can be employed to transform mediocre into magnificent. Not just playing the role of husband, but also being passionate about it. Not just being a dad, but also being a difference maker. Even in my job as a NASA scientist, I can be passionate about the safety of the Space Shuttle and astronauts as I develop new technologies. Mr. McDonald, what you gave us tonight was a path---clues to unlock excellence in magic...and life"   Frank R.

I remember thinking about that grumpy old man telling me about my lazy S speech impediment, and then I smiled.

Addressing my dyslexia.

When I wrote my first book, Born for This - Destiny Authenticated, the most common question received was how was writing a book possible being dyslexic. It was difficult; I read the draft several times. I sent copies to the people in my circle. Their job was to catch anything I didn't. From nine years old until just a few years ago, I wouldn't tell anyone. I read contracts three times. Determined to be successful in spite of learning issues, I did my best to cover it up. Now my message to individuals who have this learning issue is push through it and find a way to get around this issue. If I can do it, it can be done.

Time and space are limited as it is in this publication. If I had a little more time, I would tell you.... To Thine Own Self Be True.... you must not deceive yourself in to thinking that you are the end all be all. Never believe your own press; if you believe the good stuff that is said about you, you must believe the bad things as well. Believe in your own ability to achieve. Don't depend on people to validate you. Understand that not everyone will be happy for you. Even clowns fight, and they are the epitome of happy.

If I had just a little more time, I would also address that you should try to stand out and keep moving. Create your own paradigm shift because once you settle and begin doing what everyone else is doing, you then become part of the herd.

Finally, my most significant discovery so far in my life is that... integrity means everything - Kenrick Ice McDonald

LIVE-MORE.CA

Jonathan Tarrant

The Phoenix

By Jonathan Tarrant

What is "success"? What does that mean?

Judging your level of success will depend on your values and the lens through which you see everything.

Success to one person might mean becoming a billionaire. For them, anything less than that constitutes failure, so they might drive themselves relentlessly to achieve their vision of success, quite likely to the exclusion of everything else, such as their health, relationships, and fun. When they achieve that single minded goal, what have they really got? What then?

Success to another person may look like being able to brush his own teeth again by himself after recovering from a horrendous and debilitating accident.

Imagine how your priorities and view of success might change if you had to face your own mortality. Imagine how your perceptual lenses might change if everything you normally take for granted was suddenly taken away like your health, or your home, or the relationships you rely on.

So far, I've personally been blessed with good physical health and a surprisingly resilient mind. My mind has gone from cluttered, confused, and out of control into strong, clear, and focused. My mind and my heart have led me to a new vision of what my life can be, and I've been blessed with the inspiration and clarity which started me on the path I now walk.

My journey as an entrepreneur and as a men's self-discovery coach has been dramatic, abrupt, terrifying, exciting, challenging as hell, unexpected, beautiful, and the most wonderfully tumultuous time of my life, and I'm just getting started.

I've been through some of the most emotionally trying times. I have faced the collapse of everything I previously knew and relied on for security. I've faced my darkest fears and demons and lived to tell the tale because I'm more powerful than they are. More than that, I have come through the fire to the other side, feeling stronger than ever before and finally knowing myself for the first time in my life.

That feels like major success to me. Finally feeling as if I know who I am and knowing that I'll be fine no matter what is huge.

Now that I know the way; it's my honor to share what I've learned with other men.

It's taken a long time to get this far---longer than I would've preferred. It would've been great if I had found someone much earlier on---someone like a guide or a mentor (or a Self-Discovery Coach!) who would've recognized my pain and helped me to learn faster---to grow faster.

For the longest time, in the absence of solid guidance, I daydreamed about going on some kind of journey where I could "find myself" either by disappearing into the jungles of Brazil for a year or by dropping acid until I connected with the universe and achieved some sort of drug induced clarity. I used to feel very much like I was adrift in the world---like an observer, not really a part of anything. I always felt the presence of a massive burning desire inside my soul but had absolutely no idea of what to do with it. I always felt very disconnected from it and from myself. This sensation left me feeling constantly dissatisfied with almost everything, including me.

This was a state of mind of which I greatly underestimated the seriousness.

Having lived with my own internal monolog all my life, I was quite used to it. That monologue was always very critical of me--very judgmental and confusing. I was so uncomfortable, and yet it all felt terribly normal. As my state of mind got slowly worse, I still continued to underestimate how out of balance I was becoming.

Let's go back in time a little...

As a younger man, I learned to insulate myself from hurt by suppressing my emotions and closing myself off. Sure, I had friends and I had fun. I just learned to keep a significant portion of myself protected by never letting anyone see him. I'm an only child, and my parents moved us from house to house quite often, so I constantly had to leave my friends behind. I also feel as though I never really trusted my parents. I don't feel as if we established much of a strong bond. Especially as a teenager, I wanted desperately to be free of my mother and to be seen by my father. Neither of which were achieved in a way I'd describe as successful. I got my freedom from my mother at least, but it was not a healthy or friendly freedom for many, many years.

Suppressing my feelings, finding comfort in isolation, and not asking for help became my coping mechanisms. As I kid, I didn't know how to relax and just be me. I didn't feel as if I fit into the social expectations and male stereotypes, and I was very self-conscious. Even as I grew up and started a family of my own, these behaviors remained as a baseline. Now that I'm a father, I care deeply about raising my kids. When they were little, I wanted to give them so much and show them how to love themselves. I wanted them to be comfortable in their own skins and feel free to express their personalities. It is not easy to teach or be an example of such things when you have almost no experience with them yourself. I tried to give so much more than I actually had at that time. Life began to overtake me.

Initially, I embraced the many changes in my lifestyle. I went from a family of three (my parents and me) to a large extended family. I did my best to keep up; there were many benefits, of course. At some point early on, I began to feel as though I was disappearing. Somewhere along the way I'd lost myself and fallen into someone else's routine. When I first noticed this, I had the idea that I didn't really know or like my old self that much anyway, so maybe it wasn't such a loss. As the years went on though, it became a big problem. It became a hole that I tried to fill with external things. I looked outside of me and outside of my marriage for ways to feel better. Nothing ever worked. I never got more than temporary relief, and like a crazy person, I continued to repeat the same poor choices, hoping that eventually I might get a different result.

I always ended up feeling more lonely, more frustrated, and more gross about the way I was acting.

There was no one to talk to about it because I had secretly shut everyone out. I shut out the wife who loved me and my closest friends, who would have done just about anything for me. I was afraid to admit my deepest thoughts and fears, so they remained within me, festering. I didn't want to trouble others with my problems because I didn't feel worthy of the effort or attention. In my heart, I knew I was out of control, and I was ashamed of who I'd become. I was scared to be vulnerable. I can say that I really didn't know how to be vulnerable or open, and of course, as a man, I've been programmed to see those things as weakness.

Certainly, many other people have endured tremendous hardships and adversity in their lives. My life, when looked at from the outside, has been quite free from such obvious challenges. I've had so much good fortune and so many blessings which I've been very grateful for as much as I was able. Part of the problem was that these things made it so much harder for me to accept that I could be unhappy. What right did I have to be unhappy with my beautiful house, beautiful family, and cushy job? The biggest part of the problem was that I carried my hardships and adversities around in my head, where no-one else could see them.

I was blind to all the raging beauty and love that surrounded me. I felt small and frail, but I never showed it.

My great challenge in life has been finally to release all the conflict and pain inside myself and take responsibility for the way I allowed it to consume me. I refused to take it seriously and slowly lost myself inside of it.

Eventually, I brought about the end that I desired. I desperately wanted out of that life but couldn't bear the thought of taking the responsibility. I couldn't stand the idea of letting my family down like that, of failing, and of losing all my comforts and fending for myself. I didn't feel strong enough. Then literally overnight everything changed. The choice was made for me, which is to say that the cost of my terrible choices finally had to be paid. Everything came to a head, and I had to leave the house. In the morning, there I was in the cold of March in Toronto looking for a place to live and straining to get my head around all the consequences and challenges that were barreling towards me. All hell had broken loose, and with it, remarkably, came clarity. It was time to sink or swim.

Everything I'd been holding in for so long suddenly came gushing out all at once. All my empathy, all my love and compassion, all my deep regret and terrible pain, all my capacity for happiness and darkness, and all the strongest emotions were suddenly available to me, and honestly, I was just fucking drowning in it all for months. It took a solid couple of years to really get a handle on what to do with all these intense feelings. I can only imagine what it must have been like for my family and friends.

What I've learned to do with my emotions is give them space. I allow them to flow, and I do my best to embrace them. This is an incredibly powerful practice: learning to be accepting of your own feelings and knowing that you can handle them, knowing that they'll pass if you allow them to, and knowing that you'll be just fine.

I found incredible resilience while I was completely broken and felt as if suicide would be a welcome relief from all the pain, shame, and anxiety. I got myself through many dark days by holding on to the notion that I could choose to end it all tomorrow if I decided that I really couldn't take the weight of living anymore. It was the shock of it all and the dismay that finally opened my eyes. My old life ended so abruptly, and I could not ignore or deny the harsh reality of what I was experiencing. I could clearly see exactly how I'd brought myself to that place. Most surprising of all, amongst the overwhelming chaos and heartbreak, part of me actually felt relief.

I remember that feeling so clearly. The very next day, after getting kicked out, I was sitting in a little restaurant, eating a fresh meat pie, watching the people outside walking past the window, completely in shock, and I remember that feeling washing over me. Relief. I'd just been thrown out of my house and effectively, my life and was facing some very serious consequences... and I felt relief.

Finally, something had forced me to change. Finally, I'd gotten what I was ashamed to want most. Freedom.

I sought out some good, solid help and discarded my pride. The walls came down, and I allowed the world to see me broken. More than that, I allowed the world to see the Real me---all of me. I no longer cared to worry about the opinions of others. I no longer felt as though any of that mattered. As I slowly collected and reassembled myself, I began to reconnect with my soul and my intuition. I left out most of the parts that didn't serve me, and I questioned everything I'd ever believed about myself. So much of what I thought I knew about me had been wrong! I learned to listen deeply to my inner guiding voice---not the loud one, the quiet one, the one who takes a little practice to hear and most importantly to trust. By learning how to really listen to that guidance, I have found significant peace of mind. Instead of asking others for advice, I practice feeling the answer inside of myself. The right answer is always there, and you already know what it is.

One of the cornerstones of my success, so far, has been cultivating this relationship with my intuition---giving myself the time and the respect to get still and just feel the answer. This practice has guided me faithfully and allowed me to confidently make the choices that have served me best.

I've also learned to lean into the uncertainty of life. I embrace the adventure. I seek it, whereas before, I was increasingly averse to change and always afraid of the worst. I was afraid of the unknown and the darkness.

What is light without darkness? Both are necessary. Each gives context and power to the other. My light now shines a thousand times brighter and more clearly than ever before. The brightness I've discovered inspires and compels me to share my experience with the world, and my breakdown gave me the gift of clarity to create my brand, Live-More.

Live-More dropped out of the sky, complete, right into my mind. I remember looking up at the clouds, seeing the vision that had finally revealed itself to me and marveling at it with my mouth open. That was the rebirth of myself and the realization of my greater purpose. The Live-More platform is how I share my revelations, hard won lessons, creativity, and philosophy with the world. It was born from the super-nova that resulted from my star collapsing. That explosion opened my mind. That explosion finally awakened me to the world and to the meaning of life. That explosion freed my heart, freed the love inside of me, and created a space for me to reconnect with who I really am. The path of Live-More leads you to a deep, powerful, and wholehearted relationship with yourself and with the world.

This kind of relationship with self opens all doors to the abundance of life. More love, More connection, More confidence, More compassion, More money, Better health. There truly is no limit. To Live-More is to be free.

Live-More is a global platform which is the foundation for other projects such as my podcast and the powerful online course called "The Lost and Found Man".

This course and most of my other work are aimed squarely at men. Men don't get nearly enough support or room to be themselves, and it is high time we called bullshit on all the social stereotypes and programming. It's time for brothers to stand together and really see each other. Our social programming puts us in a behavioral box that shames us when we try to leave, so we're very inclined to keep the stereotypes going year after year---generation after generation.

The Lost and Found Man shows us that the strongest, manliest person we can ever be is ourselves fully and wholeheartedly and without shame. It guides us into that reality.

A man who's comfortable with himself, confident, and connected to his heart and able to express himself will serve his family and friends at the highest level.

My mission is to make a tremendous positive cultural change in the world, starting with men and serving all people.

This is the kind of success and generational change I'm blazing towards right now. This kind of success has meaning and real value to me and to everyone I work with.

The path I chose to follow, that got me to where I am today, was pretty awful in many ways. There were many wrong turns, many dark nights, and many times where I forgot that I was responsible for my choices. Only now have I learned that I can carve any path I want. The last few years, since I woke up, have been the most eye opening and the most beautiful time of my life. I'm actually alive now, and I no longer fear the future or look at it with a sense of dread. Despite all the incredible pain I experienced and the all the hurt that I've caused my family and my friends, the Real me has emerged like a phoenix, and I know I'm finally on course. I've finally found myself and my connection with the world.

This feels like massive success to me. From here, I can go anywhere I want. I can create anything I want. I have the tools, the confidence, the guidance, and the network.

I would love nothing more than to elevate all men to such a place.

I am the man I needed when I was younger and lost.

I am your guide and ally.

Much love.

Connect with JT:

Email: Jonathan@Live-More.ca

Get the newsletter!
https://bit.ly/TheLIVE-MORE_InsideLook

Web: www.LostAndFoundMan.ca
www.Live-More.ca

https://youtube.com/channel/UCSOkUtFwB6w4ETjduReHuhw

Socials:
https://www.facebook.com/jonathan.tarrant.3
https://www.instagram.com/live.more.ca
https://www.linkedin.com/in/jonathan-tarrant-mens-guide-live-more

Podcast: (The Path of Self Discovery with Jonathan Tarrant)
https://open.spotify.com/show/1D9fC69ytdoob4Mka2pBAj?si=4dow0-FpRJitynDD3BommQ

THE BLACK BLAZER

MEN ENTREPRENEURS "BLAZING TO SUCCESS"

Rodrick Chambers

The Journey of Cultivating Sacred Success

By Rodrick Chambers

CEO of H2O - Healing 2 Optimization LLC

Rodrick Chambers is an author. His first book was published on November 1, 2021. Rodrick is also a recording artist. Rodrick's career spans across 15 plus years as an educator and advocate for 100s of high school to college aged youth desiring access into higher education. Working with federal and state funded grants, such as TRIO Student Success (College Program), TRIO Upward Bound (Pre-College Program), Youth Employment Programs (YEP), and Community Violence Prevention Programs (CVPP), Rodrick has acquired skills in facilitating, training, and engaging students/staff in their learning experiences. This experience also has led to working overseas in Asia and Europe. Rodrick's unique academic background as a graduate from Eastern New Mexico University (ENMU) in Music (Associates), Broadcast Journalism (BS), and Mass Communication (MA) has afforded him the opportunity to participate and serve the ministry of education in innovative and creative ways through song writing, professional interviews, and advocacy for economically disadvantaged youth, and discussions with State Representatives. Rodrick's educational path continues to render new opportunities to connect students to their individual purpose(s) across the planet. In the last few years Rodrick has up-leveled his licensing and certifications in the areas of Massage Therapy and Nutritional and Transitional Coaching. He uses his new credentials to travel around the State of Texas providing therapy and educating clients on subject matters related to healing and optimizing their health.

Meaning of Success:

Much like everything around us, the meaning of 'success' has evolved over the course of my life. When I was a child, success meant purchasing a large house, having a nice car, and having a large family to live in that house. When I was a college student 'success' meant graduating, locating that dream job, and starting a family. As I have gone on to graduate with my B.A. in Communications, attain my MA in Mass Communication (not using either degree professionally), spend most of my career working in Education, live in a few different states, live outside the USA for a few years, work overseas for two different companies, and start my own businesses, my ideas about 'success' have taken on a whole new meaning.

I have grown to accept that success is relative to who and what your experiences are. A friend of mine in my travels, who is a few years older than I, coined a thought as a result of his travels to many countries and continents and living overseas; that thought was knowing when to "cash-in" and make the most of your experiences. That was over five years ago, and I still have yet to travel as much as he has and accomplish as much as he did in his travels; however, I liked the sound of "cashing-in". I may not have accomplished as much as he did, but I had acquired many successes and achievements in my own right that I know that others have benefited from.

At this time in my life, success looks like reflecting over the course of my 38 years of living and determining how to position and leverage all my life successes, while converting those successes to be of service to others; in addition to somehow creating something so encompassing of all of my human experiences that when I see the end result, it feels like one big mural, orchestra, or better yet, frozen music in motion. I sense that my company H2O - Healing 2 Optimization LLC is that step forward into 'cashing-in' and moving my 'living' 'breathing' artwork into motion.

Let me take some time to unpack some of the details of my life to explain some of my successes in a more clear and relatable way. Coming up as a troubled youth living in poverty, struggling academically, and battling many fist fights, life just wasn't a pleasant experience, overall. My parents separated at a very young age; in fact, my parents were young teenagers when conceiving my older sister and me. She and I are only nine months apart, and my parents conceived at 13 and 14 years old. Looking back, my parents truly were the hero and shero of my life. Though there were many tumultuous confrontations between the two of them, they both survived, which many have not. My mother started as an entrepreneur almost 40 years ago and has established an extremely successful career as a beautician. My father has graduated with two Masters, an extended coaching career, is approaching retirement, and has started his own entrepreneurial endeavors in the recent years. As you may have concluded, my parents and I have grown up together.

In my recently released book, Almost Doesn't Count, Or Does It?, I go into details about how the athletic discipline of my father taught me so many skills and competencies around managing hardships. Moreover, I would be remiss not to include my mother's tutelage by example and by way of the 'iron hand with the velvet glove 'guidance she provided. Quite honestly, it was more iron than velvet, in those days; however, she delivered top tier training with restricted resources and experiences. I also must sing the praises of my step-parents that joined the parenting movement in their very young or younger years with little to no training.

I am convinced that if I avoided mentioning my upbringing and my origin, it would 'mathematically' make no sense to share my experiences as an adult as well my understanding of success. The most powerful asset I have to date is my willingness to 'weave' through the chaos of my youth and make meaning out of my life presently. That my friends is success. To work through the hardships and learn the skill of alchemy by way of transmuting the hurt, bitterness, and anger into light and gold...there is little more precious than this. To then take that light and gold and create art, business, and medicine by way of information for the world around you, this is divinity. This kind of divinity is a success in the meta-realms.

I have yet to master this skill of alchemy, but I have learned to resource the light and gold of my transformation as a general map to success. I call this my blueprint to mastering all. As long as I know that I am being led by Spirit, I have no doubt that whatever I touch will be successful. Ooh! I almost forgot to mention the Spirit is the Master Teacher of alchemy without this knowledge... the process is just meaningless. Onward, the light and gold of my past has taught me to illuminate the darkness where the true treasures of life live and 'materialize' it for application purposes. What does this look like? Peace, harmony, and order.

If you stay long enough in the meta-realms of success, you will discover how your path will overlap with so many that you may or may not meet. This path will teach you the importance of humility ushering you into a more unitive consciousness---the need to know we need each other. Success is not a separatist or individualistic program alone but about how we need each other. We need each other's gifts. We need each other's love. We need each other's laughter. We need each other's friction, complication, understanding, and validation.

Success is truly a team effort. We all desire to be understood and validated, but let's make that change happen in us, first. There was a poster of insect ants in my college office as a student worker that has guided me throughout my career that sums it all up for me - "You alone have to do 'it', but you don't have to do it alone."

Advice to Others and Youth:

In considering the advice to share with others and our youth, there are a few things from my life that come to mind. There's the story of developing a passion for reading and showing yourself friendly. Let's go in order.

My Passion for Reading

One of the things I value most about my mother is her passion for reading and purchasing books for me as a child. It seems quite contradictory that I would be struggling in my youth academically but loved to read and still do. Reading was one of my escapisms from a dissatisfied childhood. It was the early birthday cards with pictures and loving words that appealed to me at an early age. It was the description about dinosaurs that exploded my imagination on unparalleled levels. Reading gave me life!

It was in my fourth-grade year that I knew I had a passion to read and write. I was pulled out of my classroom by teachers who were normally chastising me about my poor behaviors. But this time it was different. If I remember correctly, there were three teachers standing outside waiting to meet me. I was nervous, but their calm settled me to avoid thinking the worst. "Did you write this?" says one of the teachers, while holding a posterboard up with my drawing of a black young cowboy. I said yes, quite naturally. The three of them looked at each other in some disbelief, but it was the truth. But I get it; this was at the other end of the spectrum from my usual rants and fights down the hallway. The teachers continued to question me as if they were determined to confirm some foul-play in my work, but what they didn't realize was every time I read something I transcended. I soon discovered that this transcendence manifested in my writing.

The Scholastic Book Fair was one of my top three most favorite memories as a child. I got on my best behavior to receive funds to purchase at least one or two of my favorite books. Thank God, my parents did not withhold; they helped me to invest in my passion for reading. It was this investment that led to summers in my childhood of imagining, creating, and growing in my soul the possibilities of changing the landscape of my mental terrain.

All this said, please understand, I am clear that reading may not be everyone's 'thing'; however, gathering information, sitting with that information, and creating within the domains of your imagination are what I am promoting most. Whatever you are interested in, fall in love with it and cultivate it as much as you can. Let your place of 'bliss' expand. Ask yourself: how are you winning for you? How are you giving yourself a chance to live your dream? When you can not only ask yourself these questions but also live in the questions and live 'out' the questions, then you will optimize whatever path or gift you desire to see manifest.

To be straightforward, we are in the midst of re-imagining how we 'do life.' We are having to consider a new normal. We've seen so many dark days as a global community, but we've seen some of the best days, too. In the last year I have buried four relatives. All four of my paternal aunts have transcended. One of my eldest first cousins has completed his path as well. If there's one thing I have learned, while all this has happened, it's that you have to discern the times and cycles of life we are in while also discerning your 'role' in the present and what's emerging. Trust the spiritual equipment that you've cultivated along the way, so while enduring the 'dark days' you get better. From the young to the old of my relatives who died in this last year of 2020 and 2021, their lives reminded me how they lived their passion. They were successful in completing many achievements, and sadly, they were unsuccessful in achieving some achievements. Nonetheless, reviewing the collage of memories archived in a memorial program made me consider what life I will choose to live in the 'dash.' You know about the 'dash,' right? The days you have between your date of birth and your death date.

Showing Yourself Friendly

If you all can bear another one of my childhood memories... come with me down memory lane. It's the fall semester of my fifth-grade year, and we are looking at a chubby Little Rod in Miss Hill's homeroom. You may be chuckling under your breath, a bit. It's okay! I am, too. Oh, you see that, too? Yep! You are thinking why isn't Rod paying attention in class? Well, if you look a little closer, he is studying...maybe he's not studying what the Teacher has on the agenda for class, but nonetheless, he is studying. What is he studying? Let's move a little closer, so we can look over his shoulder. Is that...? "Why in the world is Rod studying that," is what you're thinking, right? You mean you've never thought about learning sign language? Of course, every child has considered learning sign language to decode what the other kids in class were saying about them.

If you look closely at the two young ladies on the opposite side of class to the left and right of the u-shaped arranged desks, you will witness them totally ignoring the teacher's math lesson for the day, too. But these two classmates are more interested in discussing and talking about Little Rod's hateful and bully type behaviors. Contrary to your belief or observations, Little Rod was aware of the hateful behaviors he developed against his classmates as well as teachers; it wasn't strange to overhear teachers discussing Rod explicitly and implicitly while enduring disciplinary reprimands outside of class or the principal's office. The two girls didn't understand the challenges of his home life, nor should they as they were dealing with their own childhood challenges. But that wasn't the point. Little Rod was dedicated to making sure that in whatever language spoken verbally or nonverbally, he wasn't going to let anyone get away with treating him so unfairly.

Oh, no! Don't turn away from Rod too quickly! Did you feel that cold chill coming from the two classmates' eyes as they discover that Little Rod just 'un-cracked' the code of what was being said about him. Wait for it...wait for it! And ka-boom! An outrageous Rod is about to give a little 'show and tell'.

Okay, guys! This is an appropriate time to exit stage left...the time portal will be returning to the present in five, four, three, two and zoom! Alright, I know that was a lot. Let's unpack that. What did you see? How did this experience make you feel? Look deeper. Ask yourself why at least five times deep. For example: I felt sad. Why? Because I didn't like the way little Rod was feeling. Why? Because he created a hostile environment for his classmates. Etc. I believe what you will discover is your experience(s) will show-up in the story. Let me provide some fillers. As a child, enduring the challenges of my upbringing made me feel isolated. I did not trust many people. Truthfully, I was full of fear. How many of our youth and adults are full of isolation, distrust, and fear? I encounter more people who claim they trust no one more than those who do. I am not recommending we blindly or foolishly trust everyone we meet, but we are gravely mistaken if we believe our journey is supposed to be some isolated, distrustful, and fearful event. Gaining friends and being friendly are truly golden rules in life.

Let's take a parenthetical break. I was watching an interview between Oprah and Maya Angelou. Maya shared a story of her son when he was a child and how he struggled during a period in gaining friends. He tells his mother that he had no friends. I paraphrase: she responds to him by asking "have you been friendly?" In his own simple way, he realizes he hadn't been much of a friend to his classmates. Sometimes we have to ask ourselves the simple but hard questions...have you been friendly?

In conclusion, success can mean so much for each of us. It is as diversified as the people we see from day to day. You have a Creator that desires to see you successful. Moreover, you have a cloud of witnesses cheering you on as you read this article and your incarnate soul has already identified the winner in you.

Have you been trustworthy? Have you provided a safe place around you that draws others to you? The answers to these questions may get you closer to building the kind of friendships you desire---in fact, the kind of relationships that you need. Consider, if you resonate in the frequency of trust, peace, and friendliness, that is what you will get in return. The way this universe works is what you sow is what you reap. We understand that the karmic cycle renders what we give out. It may take time...process...cycles to reap your harvest, but you will gain the kind of relationships you have sowed into.

Isolation, distrust, and fear are part of the process, but they are not conclusive. The moments of experiencing these things should prompt you to pulsate more of the love, peace, and drive to make life better. If you don't possess these things, meditate and/or study to bring these things into your life.

I must share with you that during that fifth-grade year I was able to show myself friendly in moments that I began to gain the trust of my classmates. It still took time before my friendship with those two young ladies improved. It was consistently convincing them that I wasn't going to attack them but cherish their friendship as well as their ability to be forgiving and kind. For the rest of my junior high and high school years, those two young ladies became dear to me, and we would consult and console each other during our high school years.

Trust me, every story doesn't end so happily, but it was good to know that some principles can work themselves out in real-time and while you are alive. But we can't allow what doesn't work to overshadow our progress.

In conclusion, success can mean so much for each of us. It is as diversified as the people we see from day to day. No matter what your success definition is or what your success story is not, choose to make a difference, starting now. Put it in your psyche that change is possible and that you can do anything you put your mind to. Your mind is the crowned glory of All, Universe... God; your mind is the access into all that exists. Located in your mind is no space or time but the essence and power of creativity. You have a Creator that desires to see you successful. Moreover, you have a cloud of witness that is cheering you on as you read this article and your incarnate soul has already identified the winner in you. So, the only thing left to do is believe and move it into your actions, daily.

Remember, cultivate your passions. Get to know who you are. What kinds of gifts you possess. What you like most. What you do not like. If you don't gather information about anything else... learn your habits. Research why you do what you do and how you do it. Also, bear in mind that this journey of success... life... is not just about you! Serve someone else. Be kind and friendly to someone. Someone needs your smile. Your hug. Your eye contact. Your presence and your ability to be present.

Joseph Boy

Take your kid to work day SUCKS!!!
By Joseph Boy

Well, this is an interesting story. Joe Boy is a computer tech in Central Florida, and he has always wanted to be a father. He was determined to be a great dad. He had inspiration from a song he has heard, "Cat's in the Cradle" from Harry Chapin. This song was a poem that Harry's wife had written to show what could happen if you get so busy with life. It is a heartbreaking song about a father and son that can never schedule time to spend with each other. Joe Boy was going to use this as motivation to ensure he spends time with his son and helps him be the best man he can be and in turn do the same for his children. To this end, Joe Boy loved taking his son to work and showing him all the computers and the parts and cool buttons everywhere. Tiberius always had fun there and showed lots of interest. Over time Joe taught him how to build a computer from the bottom up and discovered that Tiberius really did not enjoy it. He did enjoy visiting customers and talking with them. This was great because Joe could fix the client computer while Tiberius kept them entertained.

One day Joe is working on a computer in a radio studio and Tiberius starts to play with the microphones. Joe corrects him and tells him not to touch them because he did not want to have to replace them. The studio owner encouraged Tiberius to play and asked what he would talk about. So far Tiberius has not stopped talking yet. After making a makeshift show they were told to come by the next week. Each week the show got better and faster to produce. Tiberius wanted to interview people about their jobs and what people did for their passion. This was instilled into him at a young age when he was learning to read. Joe would walk him around downtown showing him all the signs around asking him to read them. He would say the name and then Joe would ask "What does that sign mean?". So, Tiberius would say Publix and that is where you get food. When Tiberius did not know what it meant, like for the sign ACCOUNTING, he was told to go inside and ask them what they do. The people usually would sit with him and explain a little about their job and what they did for a living. This lesson would end up being the cornerstone of the content of his radio show.

Tiberius also added stuff he learned from school like being LION Strong. This was having the virtues of Leadership, Integrity, Obedience, and Nobility. Each one he would describe and how he saw it used during the week. After a few months Joe Boy realized he needed to build a studio. He altered his office and built a full studio for Tiberius to record his show. He started to call radio stations and would send them a copy of the show and ask them to air it. After the first one said yes, they wanted a very large fee. This was the realization that they needed to get sponsors. So Joe took Tiberius to a number of clients to go ask them to be a sponsor and learn how to run his show like a business. Each "yes" was celebrated with a root beer, and each "no" would be cried over at home. But money was raised, and he was on the radio. Then came the realization that to do a good show you have to have a continued supply of guests. Joe had not only to run the computer company but also produce a radio show and find a guest each week. Joe would call everyone he knew to be guests and talk about their jobs. Tiberius got to interview the headmaster of his school, the captain of the Jamaican bobsled team, and newscasters from the local TV stations.

Each week Tiberius would need to read a book and review it. This was a great way to keep him reading. He also would play a new video game and review it for the show. This would force creative writing skills that would help in his development. Everyone thought that Joe was crazy. He had slowed down his business to give more time to work with Tiberius and his show, and it was not making any money. It was not losing money, but it was not generating an income. Each time he was asked about this, Joe would simply say this was about Tiberius getting an education that you can't get anywhere else, and it allowed him to have productive way to spend time with his son. Tiberius was learning lots of life lessons and was getting to meet tons of people all over the world. He got to remotely interview a podcast host in Pakistan, Dr. Carl Wilson the author of this book, and even the greatest bowler in the world, Jason Belmonte. Joe was learning as well. He was getting better at producing a show and even started video production. His computer clients would ask his to produce promos and shows for them allowing to raise the funds to get better equipment.

Joe is a member of Rotary and instills in Tiberius the four-way test. First, is it TRUTH? Second, is it FAIR to all concerned? Third, will it build GOOD WILL and BETTER FRIENDSHIPS? Fourth, will it be BENEFICIAL to all concerned? Then they added a fifth one. Is it FUN? This was very important when building the radio show. It was about sharing the virtues of LION Strong and all the possible jobs in the world. Most children are taught about being a policeman or astronaut. But Tiberius wanted to show all the other jobs, like mortgage broker, real estate, even house cleaner. By using the four-way test learned from Rotary they were able to ensure to keep journalism integrity and put out a quality show while learning about media. Joe has won several awards but don't ask him to list them. He doesn't look for a pat on the back, and you will only find one on his wall. Tiberius has learned that the sheets of paper are not valuable, but the journey and skills that are earned are important.

So what is the one that he does display? Well in his home he has a thank you poster signed by a number of kids from the Boys and Girls Club. Joe started an organization teaching kids how to repair computers. Each time a client would buy a new computer he would give him the old one to get rid of. Joe would provide those computers for kids to learn on. They would take them apart and rebuild them. After they were working, he would donate them to non-profits and clubs that worked with children. All he would ask in return was a letter stating how the computer would be used for good. He would share the letter with the client that gave him the computer in the first place. After building a computer lab made from the donated computers, the kids at the Boy and Girls Club surprised him by making a poster, and all the kids signed it.

Joe and Tiberius play video games together and have lots of fun building things in Minecraft as well as blowing stuff up in Overwatch. Each game is another opportunity for a lesson and ability to review something new for his radio show. Joe really likes real time strategy games because they teach things like resource management and risk versus reward. Joe has been playing video games ever since he was kid himself and ran a local lanparty letting local children play games on computers that he provided. It would be normal to have a weekend with 30 teens at the house playing games till two in the morning. He encouraged educational games instead of shoot 'em up games and team-based shooters instead of all for one. He has banned a few games from Tiberius. It is important to enjoy saving the hostage or helping the team versus running over people or causing pain. Joe believes that parents should take the time to play with their children and even learn video games so they can better understand the world as they see it.

Joe believes that the most important asset people have is their knowledge and the people they have around them. If you surround yourself with positive people and share your knowledge freely with them, everyone will build each other up and grow together. Tiberius in a way is a product of that concept. Teaching kids about computers and how to build them was a way to help them be off the streets and give them something to do that was productive. Every once in a while, Joe will get a phone call or email from a kid who had been playing video games at his house and learned to build computers. The kid is no longer a kid but an adult with children of their own. They tell stories of the past and how much it was an influence on their lives to learn about computers and develop a love for learning more. They are teaching their children the same skills and showing them to share with others. This is the full circle that helps a village raise a child to be an adult.

So this year Joe learned a hard lesson. He learned about his mortality. COVID has been all over the news for a while, and well, he got it in July. He was hospitalized for two weeks. During that time, he thought about all the lessons that he would not get to share with his son. At one point he was on a video call with Tiberius, and the alarms started to go off. His oxygen level had gone from 98 to 88. Then to 76 then to 70. Tiberius asked what the noise was, and Joe just said to keep telling him about the video game he was playing. Joe was listening seeing his life leaving him. He thought he was going to die. As the meter dropped past 65, he thought at least he would die watching his son that he was so proud of. Then he thought of how selfish that was. But enjoying his last moments watching his son was also ensuring that Tiberius's last memory of his father would be his death. With that he told Tiberius that he needed to disconnect the call to deal with something with the nurses. Tiberius was not happy to lose the call but said he understood. Right after the call was disconnected, the nurses arrived to assist.

Two weeks in the hospital and Joe was one of forty that was released that day. He was so happy to be able to hug his son and know that he would be able to continue to teach him valuable lessons that he could carry on to his children one day. What was the first lesson he wanted to teach him? Well, he pulled up a website and searched for a video. They sat down together and listened to "Cat's In The Cradle" and talked about its meaning and why it is so important to enjoy every moment you have with each other because you never know when it will be all gone.

If you want to listen to the radio show/podcast, be sure to look up "The Tiberius Show" on YouTube and subscribe to his channel. He has a website and Facebook page as well. If you want to be a guest, contact Joe and tell him what you do for a living. You can find Joe fixing computers or producing shows at his office at Your Computer Solutions Inc. But remember to look around you and see the positive people in your life. Thank them and share your knowledge with them freely. Instead of just looking for fun things to do, look for productive things you can do with your children and make them fun.

So, what will they do next? Well Joe and Tiberius are working on a talk. The subject is this: Take your kid to work day and how maybe it should not only be one day a year. You should spend "sharing" time with your kid every day you can; this will create amazing results not only in your relationship but in your child's development and growth. You will get to learn so much about what your child really enjoys and what is really going on in his world. Joe and Tiberius hope to do their talk at the Rotary Club and other social club events spreading the message to take your kid to work as well as LION Strong. You never know maybe one day you will see them on a TED Talk stage.

Photo credit: Mark Cunningham

Darryl K. Horton

Walking Miracle

By Darryl K. Horton

I rebuilt my Life after Life as I knew it was gone.

At the age of five was my first surgery on my ankle. I remember the doctor telling me I would never walk normally. The next two years were spent in leg braces to help me not walk on my toes. Challenges became a part of life. Due to the surgery, my left leg is about two inches shorter than the right leg.

I am the son of a Vietnam Veteran, a career Marine for 22 years. Being a teenager, we, of course, had our disagreements although without a doubt, I wanted to be like him, compassionate and inspirational---an influencer and strong. I did not realize how much I embodied those attributes until my health crisis occurred.

I have a very high pain threshold, but on May 11, 2016, I was tested to my limit. I woke up that morning and felt a pain different from any other I had felt in twenty-five years. I managed to make my way to the emergency room. I was only going to get something to relieve the pain. When I arrived at the emergency room, the nurse met me at the door with a wheelchair. That was 11:30 a.m.; I never left the hospital.

After two MRI'S and a CAT scan, the on-call neurosurgeon came in at 9:00 p.m. and told me he could not allow me to go home. I needed emergency surgery immediately. He cleared his schedule and performed the surgery the next morning. After a 10 ½ hour procedure, I woke up with three metal bars and screws in my back from T-2 to T-10. Yes, that strength kicked in, and I needed it to endure my journey to come. When I woke up, I had two doctors in my room, my neurosurgeon and an infectious disease specialist. My neurosurgeon told me I had no disk between my 5th and 6th vertebrae, and my spine was compressing; the infectious disease specialist told me I had Coccidioidomycosis (Valley Fever).

Talk about a one two punch---I was overwhelmed. The strength and determination I had to draw on was huge, much like the same as when I became an entrepreneur. People told me not to do it; you'll never make it. Not truly understanding the journey, I realized that I would only recover and get stronger from my efforts, mindset, and determination. As the saying goes "If it's meant to be, it's up to me". I had to set my daily goals and stay focused. I got up against the doctor's advice and stood up, telling myself "Here we go". If I can stand, I can walk; if I can walk, I can do anything I want. I thrive and strive every day to be and do more than the day before.

The next three years I needed all the strength I had, first of all, to learn to walk again and endure all the challenges: physical therapy, monthly blood draws, and doctors' appointments along with the adjustments needed that I had to face, both personally and professionally. Even with all the challenges I face now, I have been blessed to have the right doctors, nutrition, facilities, and determination available to assist in my recovery.

Even though I'm not where I want to be yet, my journey has taught me so much about myself. I started going to networking events again and rebuilding my relationships. Always show up and look for the nuggets that you'll be able to take away. I received a message from someone I didn't know at the time, who wanted to meet me and hear my story. After meeting Mary Hang, we became true friends, and she first told me she was going to help me. Unbeknownst to me Mary was the Marketing Director for Life by Design Magazine. I became a contributing writer for the magazine, which gave me a platform to help others and the knowledge and experience of writing. The opportunity was bigger than I thought; we had launch parties monthly which made it possible for me not only to meet but also to build relationships with many of the influential people on the cover of the magazine.

While attending one of our networking events, it was the start of building a relationship with Les Brown, Jr. and eventually finding out he was starting a new program called "It's Your Time Academy". I was apprehensive at first because knowing that I had very little savings left, the cost was a concern, so I just started telling myself: I'm going to do this; I'm going to do this. After saying this a few times, I realized that the academy would be a major start to my life relaunch. Then faith and fate stepped in, and Les Brown, Jr. announced that for everyone at the event, he was going to allow us to join the "It's Your Time Academy" for $99.00 a month. I could swing that for sure. I soon added Les Brown, Jr. as one of my mentors, which, of course, led to hours of one-on-one conversations and invitations to private events. The bonus was that we were all the beneficiary of Les Brown, Sr., who was also mentoring us in the academy.

After building our relationship and rebuilding my own confidence level, I decided I would relaunch my Juice Plus business in January of the following year, which was put on hold for a couple of years after surgery. Using the tools and knowledge I learned in the It's Your Time Academy, I was able to relaunch my Juice Plus business and keep it qualified for the entire year. I have been blessed with opportunities to do more.

Soon after completing the academy, I was chosen to be on the cover of the *Life by Design Magazine* for which I was a contributing writer. This led to a platform for me to be able to start living and building on my passion and purpose. You see my life was no longer about me and has never been. I have always been in a position as a facilitator, trainer, or mentor being able to share my knowledge with others. I then met my next mentor in my journey Tom Gay.

Again, being in the room, Tom approached me and told me about an event he was having in the San Diego area. I showed up, and after having a short conversation with Tom, he told me, "When you decide what it is you truly want to do, we are going to help you." We have been talking and building a relationship since that day. Tom recently launched a new networking platform TribeUp.com. He asked me to be a part of the development team. The opportunities didn't stop once I completed my profile on TribeUp. I reconnected with a business associate that I didn't realize had a radio show in the Chicagoland area, TalkZone.com. She wanted to have me be a guest on her show. My gratitude and appreciation were overflowing. After recording my segment for her show, I received a message from a friend I worked with during my 35-year career in the foodservice industry. You see, because of my injuries, I'm now 100% disabled or as I say limited.

Jace Martin had an offer for me. He asked me to partner with him and his wife to open a restaurant. The Cajun Country Cafe came to life. My passion and purpose were gaining momentum. I now have Juice Plus, Send Out Cards, Cajun Country Cafe, and a consulting business, and I'm mentoring business owners. However, it definitely didn't end there; through TribeUp.com I met a built a relationship with Denisa Gokovi, who later informed me that she and her family were starting a media company in Albania and wanted to feature my story in one of their publications *Heidens Magazine*, a recently released book *The Book of Men 2021* and a book to be released in December 2021 *Iconic Influencers of Asesthetics International 2020*. Then came a message from Australian Dr. Vicky Omifolaji with an invitation to join The Global Achievers Club.

All these opportunities led to what is truly important to me, meaningful relationships worldwide. We started an Appreciation Gratitude Movement through one of my entities. We are able to send birthday, anniversary, condolence, and many other kinds of cards worldwide celebrating important moments in other's lives and showing appreciation and gratitude. Through showing Appreciation and Gratitude, I was notified that I was nominated to be part of the Black Blazers' Organization and book. The blessings continue every day. Now I truly enjoy life and live my life by something my dad used to always say " Let your works speak louder than your material possessions.

Take time to live in the moment. The journey I thought I was on before my surgery has so much more meaning. Life had not ended; it was just beginning.

Pivot in the business world means to shift to a new strategy, sometimes drastically changing the business plan. Part of being a successful entrepreneur is having a plan to pivot and knowing the right time to pivot. With the situation happening in the world right now, so many of us have had a shock to everything we do in life. Even though for entrepreneurs our families come first, our businesses are our second families. Pivoting is essential for both of these to survive. As an entrepreneur you can't be single minded. You must use face to face meetings, when possible, business cards, and networking meetups. We must be able not only to anticipate our clients and customers' needs but also those of our employees and associates.

Over the last months a large percentage of businesses both large and small are being affected. Some are for obvious reasons, and then there are those business owners and entrepreneurs that just didn't have a pivoting plan to turn to. Pivoting and being ready to pivot at any time should be an essential part of your business plan with the use of the internet, social media, and so many different applications available to you today.

Ask yourself these questions knowing that the fact that using social media could reach over a billion people: Do you have a plan to make social media beneficial to your business? Knowing that we can no longer really have face to face meetings, are you familiar with online applications and other more efficient options? (Virtual Business Cards, Zoom, Skype Social Media Business Page). Preparation to pivot is essential; you must have the plan in place in case you need to use it. Strategies are part of business and part of being a successful entrepreneur.

The most important question is this: Do you have a Pivoting Plan in your business plan?

Making a commitment involves dedicating yourself to something, like a person, cause, or a business. We all have had to make commitments throughout our lives. From the time we were born whether we knew it or not, we were committed to learning the basics of walking, talking, and eating. In school we had a commitment to learning what we needed to advance to the next grade. When we got our first job, it was really the first time many of us truly realized what commitment. Without commitment there was very little chance we would be able to advance to the next position or be considered for advancement.

As an entrepreneur, before you make a commitment, think carefully; it becomes your obligation not only to yourself, but also to all the people associated with your business. Your employees, clients, customers, and vendors will be affected by the level of commitment you as the owner are showing. When making a decision to become an entrepreneur, your commitment will be the biggest you will make through all the commitments you may have had to make.

Yes, planning, hiring, training, and supporting are all important, especially as a business owner, because the majority of your energy and focus will be on promoting your product or service. Although as business owners we always need to realize that regardless of how impressive our company may be, there is a large percentage of possible clients or customers that may be waiting to approach us because they are waiting to see how committed we are not only to the success of our business but how committed we are to customer service, follow-up, and customer appreciation.

Commitment involves dedicating yourself to your business and all it takes to make it a success. There will be several challenges as an entrepreneur.

Will your commitment be up to the challenge?

My journey and experiences in life have allowed me to have a unique understanding. I now get to live in my Passion and Purpose- -helping others go after their dreams and being a mentor to others.

Terrance Leftridge

Terrance "The Unstoppable Coach" Leftridge
By Terrance Leftridge

Terrance is a Certified Life Accountability Coach. He is the founder of UnStopABLE Coaching Services Inc. where the #1 Goal is to help his clients FOCUS more on what they are ABLE to do and less on what is STOPPING them! He does that by partnering with them on their journey to creating, implementing, and achieving their visions.

He has worked with men and women who are transitioning from working traditional jobs and has helped them start successful careers in entrepreneurship. He teaches them how to be better marketers and better networkers and how to build stronger relationships that lead to greater exposure and more sales!

He utilizes his internet broadcast, "The UnStopABLE Stories Show with Terrance Leftridge" as a platform to expose his guests to a larger audience and, as a result, increase their circle of influence and generate leads. Terrance also uses his "UnStopABLE Author Showcase" program to help new and seasoned authors to showcase their books, causes, and upcoming events. Terrance has helped over 17 people become new authors and bring awareness to causes such as Autism, Cancer, Domestic Violence, and formerly incarcerated citizens recidivism.

He has spoken at Live and virtual seminars and training events across the country. He has been the emcee for numerous events on LIVE stages as well as virtual ones, most notably events featuring Dr. Ruben West and the Legendary Les Brown. He has hosted events, including "Unleash Your Unstoppable Purpose" in 2017 and "Real Men Speak Summit" in 2020.

For more information on booking Terrance for your next event or speaking engagement, contact him at Tleftridge@unstoppablecoaching.com.

Be A.B.L.E. to Account for Your Abilities

Hey, Hey, it's an #UnStopABLE Day. I'm here to let you know that "You Are A.B.L.E." and that makes you Unstoppable but only if you choose to be Accountable to your Abilities!

My name is Terrance "The UnStopABLE Coach" Leftridge. I am an Accountability Coach, International Speaker, Certified Virtual Presenter and Emcee, and the host of two internet weekly broadcasts. I wasn't always all the things I mentioned above. As a matter of fact, for most of my adult life, I was a criminal that had just not been caught!

Now before you call 911 and try to collect some kind of reward, let me explain. You see I was not living up to the GOD given abilities I received as a gift at birth. If I were to be arrested and forced to stand in front of a judge, I would have been convicted of "Living an Average Life!"

You know the life I'm talking about:

Getting Up

Going to Work

Coming Home

Eating dinner

Going to bed

Getting up the next day. And so on, and so on. Raise your hand if this sounds like your life as well (no one is watching but you). Are you living or are you merely existing? Are you counting the seconds of life when you should be making the seconds count?

Could you possibly be committing the same crime I would have been convicted of if I had not made a change in the nick of time?

I have found over the years of learning from my failures as well as my successes that the difference between living an "average" life and living an "UnStopABLE" life simply comes down to two things. They are what you are ABLE to do and what you are Willing to do.

The dictionary defines abilities as a talent, skill, or proficiency at a particular thing. It also refers to a person who is in possession of a skill or talent. So, when you are in "possession" of a skill or a talent, you own it. Ownership comes with a responsibility on how you use that skill or talent because you become accountable for how you use it.

So how do "UnStopABLE People" account for their abilities? In this chapter, I will touch on four principles I use daily to be accountable for my abilities. These principles help me FOCUS more on what I am ABLE to do and less on what may be STOPPING me from living life to the fullest and walking in my purpose. Get your pen and paper because I am sure these principles will help you as well to be #UnStopABLE

Principle #1 - Be Accountable for your ACTIONS

For many years, I ignored my abilities or even denied them. I was slow to develop my abilities in part because I refused to TAKE ACTION in learning what they were. When you're just existing, it isn't important to ACT. You just REACT to life as it comes your way.

Reflect on this next story and see if it resonates with anything in your life.

I worked as a Child Advocate for a social service agency for ten years. In the beginning, I was excited because I thought I was helping kids and families, but I quickly learned I was just pushing papers from one pile to the other. I was not really making a difference or tapping into my GOD given gifts, but the paycheck was good at the time, and that was enough for a while.

But then the awakenings in the middle of the night started to occur. Once a week and then two or three times each week, I would be shaken out of my dreams. The dreams would give me "coming attractions "speaking on stages, giving advice to individuals or talking people through their problems. As much as I would try to forget them and fall back asleep, those dreams followed me to work, and I began to daydream about doing more than I was currently doing. I yearned to help people in a more direct way. I had a VISION of being more, doing more, and having more.

Have you had those type of dreams? Dreams that shake you to your core? Dreams that would let go of you until you do something about them? Dreams that force you to ACT?

That was me. I soon learned the Principle of ACTION. It says that "a Vision without Action will always remain a Dream."

Remember when we used to go to the movies (I'll wait....it may be hard to remember). Before the movie started, you would be treated to clips of "coming attractions"---movies coming in the future. These clips were shown to intrigue you, tease you, and excite you enough so that you would TAKE ACTION and make plans to comeback when the movie premieres.

When you TAKE ACTION on your Dreams, you intrigue, tease, excite, and engage your abilities in the same way. The dream gives you a sneak peak of what's possible in your life. Now you become Accountable to activating those abilities in YOU to make the dream a reality!

For many of you, seeing the dream is all you will need to go out and #BeUnStopABLE! But for me and far too many people I've coached over the years, we need to embrace the 2nd principle and "Be Accountable to Believing in self.

Principle #2: Accountable to Believing in Self

Growing up as a kid, I shared a house with my mom, three siblings, my grandmother, great grandmother, and one of my aunts, affectionately called Tee. While all my relatives encouraged me to be my best, my grandmother and Tee would prophecy over my future. My grandmother thought I'd be a great actor like John Wayne, and she even gave me his nickname, the DUKE! My aunt felt I was very smart and told me I could be the "next Thurgood Marshall", the first black Supreme Court Justice.

These were both wonderful people to be like at the time, and they truly believed it for me. I, however, was not convinced. I saw other people over time that I wanted to be like, but here's the problem. I never believed I could be them or be like them. So instead, I continued to exist. Someone reading this knows what I am talking about.

You're struggling to find your own identity. As Cicone Prince says, you are waiting to be "introduced to yourself!" You have not personally developed your abilities to the point where you BELIEVE you can be whoever you wish to be. Therefore, you haven't TAKEN ACTION on becoming UnStopABLE!

The good news is that it is not too late. You still have time! You are still A.B.L.E. to develop your abilities and strengthen that belief muscle. Once you figure out what you believe in, you will take actions to place some purpose behind those beliefs.

Before I could believe in myself and my abilities, I had to invoke the 3rd principle into the formula. That is Learning from my Life Lessons.

Principle #3: Learn from Your Life Lessons

In this life, it isn't what you learn from the success as much as you learn from your failures. To learn your abilities, you must go thru some experiences. There is a quote that says, "You must go thru to grow thru." That simply means you must have all types of experiences in order to learn what your abilities and capabilities are. This is taught to you thru trials and triumphs. The trials "test" you. The triumphs "bless" you. In either case, they leave an imprint on your memory to be stored for later use.

I didn't learn I had a passion for driving until I learned how to drive. I didn't know I would excel in marching band in high school until I failed at sports. I didn't know I was called to serve on a higher level until I was fired from my good government job. In all the examples, I had to go through the life lesson and then learn what I was able to do as a result. Your life lessons have molded and shaped you since you were born and will continue to do so until you expire.

Just look at how many new abilities were found in people as a result of COVID-19. People everywhere learned new skills and discovered new and/or never used before abilities to make it through this pandemic. Some used their abilities to make a difference in the lives of others.

So how can you use the Principle of Life Lessons learned to increase your belief in yourself and move you to take action? First, take action by reflecting on the lessons of your life. Many times, when we just exist, instead of live, we don't take the time to reflect. I often heard my elders say, "If it had not been for the Lord on my side, where would I be?" In those moments, they reflect on their lives and take stock of the lessons learned and the abilities they've acquired. In those moments, they learned what they were ABLE to do because they remembered what they had been through. Because they learned the lessons from the past, it becomes easier to practice the 4th Principle: Accountable for Expecting Success.

Principle #4: Accountable for Expecting Success

I started this article with my infamous greeting, "It's an UnStopABLE Day!" For me, it is not just a greeting. It's an expectation. It's a Declaration! It's my statement to the world of the success I expect every day. I wake up saying it; then at the end of the day, I reflect on it.

I have made an expectation of success a way of life. No matter if the day brings me Obstacles or Opportunities, I know I will not be STOPPED because I have already declared that it would be an #UnStopABLE day. I have chosen, i.e., taken action, to ensure my day will be the best it can be. I chose to believe that it will be an #UnStopABLE day. After each day, I can reflect on a day where I was not stopped and use that life lesson to push me further. I know I am ABLE to be more, do more, and have more because I have a life lesson to remind me. Now it becomes easier to Expect Success because I have had success.

So now, it's your turn to use the formula in your own life. Here it is again:

Actions + Belief + life lessons learned = Expected Success

When you decide to become Accountable to following the formula, you become ABLE to have more, do more, and be more. You have the ABILITY to Not Be Stopped and that makes you #UnStopABLE!

If by chance this all sounds good, but you don't know how to get started implementing the formula, I would love to become your Accountability Coach and Partner. There is an African proverb that says, "if you want to go fast, go alone. If you want to go far, go with a team". I am willing, able, and available to partner with you on your journey to Unstop Ability... (yes, it is a word).

Let's start the journey together. Go to my GET STARTED Page at https://unstoppablecoaching.com. Or you can feel free to email me at Tleftridge@unstoppablecoaching.com

Whichever way you choose to reach me, remember YOU ARE A.B.L.E to live your life on the next level of your Greatness! Don't let anyone or anything stop from being accountable to turning your dreams into realities.

Wherever you are in the world today, don't just make it a great day. Make it an UnStopABLE day!

Terrance Leftridge
Your Accountability Coach
UnStopABLE Coaching Services

Follow me on social media
FB: @unstoppablecoaching.com
IG: @unstoppablecoaching
YouTube: www.youtube.com/TerranceLeftridge

Catch my video podcasts
UnStopABLE Stories Show: bit.ly/unstoppablestories
Talking Small Business with Terrance: bit.ly/TSBTL

UnStopABLE Coaching Services

"Coaching that helps YOU Be Accountable to Living the Life YOU were created to Live!"

Dr. Hassan Younes

PROGRESS NOT REGRESS

By Dr. Hassan Younes

Anyone wishing to become a successful entrepreneur needs to accept the constant challenges of his career of being a successful entrepreneur. It takes persistence and intense focus to push on, but that inner power can get depleted fast, draining your motivation and making it hard to stay on top.

Entrepreneurship is a journey filled with ups and downs. Both can take their toll, but what sets those that succeed apart from others is their mindset.

Richard Branson saw everyday challenges as a source of motivation, taking the opportunity to learn something new from every experience. Oprah Winfrey made a point of not limiting her belief in what's possible, and Steve Jobs was aware of the limited time we have in this world and how precious it is to use it in following our hearts and intuition.

There are many ways to revitalize your entrepreneurial spirit and keep moving forward, exemplified by the most successful leaders. Different people discover motivation in different places, but some universal methods are certain to work for most.

As entrepreneurs, we all start out with grand visions of building huge and successful companies. That vision drives us to succeed, and we put everything that we have into leading our business.

The success comes.

And that's when things start to get a little more dangerous.

Some leaders start sitting back and reaping the fruits of their labors. You've pushed so hard to get to this point that you feel as if you've earned it, and you have. However, spending too long on celebrating your success can cause you to lose focus. The drive that got you to where you are disappears, and you become a less effective leader.

You become complacent, and your business suffers as a result. It is not just your business that is at risk of collapsing.

When left unchecked, complacency can completely change who you are and what you do both in your professional and personal life. In this chapter I will talk about the dangers behind this notorious complacency factor or 'quicksand' and share with you why complacency can destroy your life and provide helpful tips on how to avoid it.

Staying in your comfort zone does not sound so bad, does it? You are in your lane, and it feels safe to stick to things that you're good at. You may have had big dreams in college, but now you're perfectly comfortable with where you are at.

However, people often don't realise that this comfort zone is what prevents you from progress in your business or personal life. Once people feel as if they've achieved their personal goals, they tend to stop pursuing new experiences. This can make them miss out on many life opportunities. This is precisely what complacency looks like, just for a start. Complacency is like quicksand that pushes you further down.

Complacency in your business and in your personal life kills. I discovered this very thing with my own business. In 2012, I was operating an expanding childcare business. It was the prime of my life as an entrepreneur as cash flow in this business was pouring in streams. The best part was that I was able to keep the business running even if I was not physically there. Our operations grew bigger and bigger, and I was satisfied---maybe excessively so--- until I just took everything for granted.

Since everything was going well, I relaxed. I let others run the business for me and indulged myself to be lazy. I even started having four-day weekends...because why not? Until suddenly, my business hit rock bottom.

From 95% business capacity and income flow, my business plummeted to a mere 34% capacity. This was below the break-even line of 45%. All in a snap.

Things got so rough that I couldn't even pay invoices just to keep the business afloat. I found no other contingency but to borrow $340,000 from elsewhere just to keep our business operation afloat.

I found that risking my family's security was the only way my business could survive. Terrible, isn't it?

It came to the point where I was afraid to answer phone calls knowing that creditors were chasing me for their money. My morale and self-esteem dropped to the lowest point in my life.

But that's not the end of it. Here's the straw that broke the camel's back:

One time, my eight-year daughter came to me and asked for a dollar for lunch as we did not have food in the house. I was so broke that I could not even give her a single dollar coin---not even after searching all over our house for one dollar. I had to send my daughter to school without food or a lunch order. I felt totally heartbroken sending my daughter to her class knowing she would be hungry that day.

I felt powerless---as if I was just going to drop dead at any time—from shame, guilt, and yes, hunger.

The complacency 'quicksand' spread across multiple domains in my business, ranging from my professional relationships, health, and even my marriage and family life.

Thankfully, I made it out of that situation alive after stepping back into my business and starting from scratch. I got myself out of the mess I made and survived by going straight to the root cause of the tragedy: the cancer of complacency.

Within a twelve-month period, I was able to turn my business around and take it back to success and achieve a business capacity of 113%.

Our businesses today have grown and multiplied threefold across multiple continents.

I'm telling you all these because the mistakes I made are the same mistakes you can make both in your business or personal life. At least, you have my experience from which to learn.

So, I will now unpack all the mistakes I made due to complacency and show you how you should avoid them. This way, you can spare yourself the heartbreaking sight of your daughter staring you in the eye when you're about to lose everything.

Here are the five ways that complacency can destroy your personal life.

Mistake #1 – You Become Resistant to Change and Fall Behind

There is a saying that goes "change is the only thing constant in this world". Ever since the dawn of time, all species have been adapting to changing environments. Those who failed went extinct eventually. Unfortunately, complacency tends to make people resistant to change. It's a matter of time before somebody complacent starts to fall behind those friends and colleagues who manage to avoid the quicksand.

Complacency makes it hard to change just about anything. Let's use an example in life. It's easy to believe in your ability to lose weight once you decide to do it. The truth is that the longer you put your health on suspension, the harder it gets to fix. You end up piling on those extra kilos that you never really shed. Habits become incredibly hard to change as we age. Since you're not getting any younger, you might as well start now.

Mistake #2 – You Start Settling

When you become complacent, you stop pushing hard or aiming for bigger things in life. Instead of shooting for lifestyle goals that make you happier and healthier, you start settling for whatever you have and become comfortable with mediocrity. You may lead a more sedentary lifestyle, read less, and eat more highly processed foods that have lower nutritional value. Before you know it, laziness takes over your life.

This is the ultimate success destroyer as it leaves no room for progress.

Mistake #3 – You Replace Good Habits with Bad Ones

Since we were children, we've invested a lot of time and effort into developing good habits. Unfortunately, it's much easier to break a good habit than to build one. As you become complacent, not only do you lose your good habits, you'll also be developing some bad ones.

Your old mindset that had a knack for making good choices is now replaced with one that can't resist temptation.

This is a big reason why being complacent is dangerous. Once you get to that phase, it becomes tough to make positive changes. The longer you remain there, the harder it is to get out.

Mistake #4 – You May Stop Making New Connections

As you become complacent, you're likely to stop making an effort to build new connections. People usually appreciate it when you show effort to earn their interest and trust. Failing to do so can cause people to want to do the same and lose whatever interest they may have had in you.

In fact, an important step on your path to success is networking, both in your personal and professional life. You put effort and time into understanding the ins and outs of your field and meet people in other companies and positions or even cities. As you become complacent, you simply stop expanding your social circle.

Worst of all, you may even lose your existing connections. As we age, we can take people in our surroundings for granted. We continue to live our lives and believe that our close friends will always remain so. Soon, you may reach a point where you only get in touch once every two months, then maybe once a year, until you only see these people at weddings and funerals.

Mistake #5 – You Stop Believing in Yourself

One of the saddest effects of complacency is losing faith in yourself. You'll look back on the past and stop believing in hard work. As you lose motivation to strive for better, your progress stops, and you no longer develop yourself as a person.

What happens next is that you're going to start noticing all these other people that are doing their job better than you. It is they who rise to the heights that you fervently dreamed about. At that point, you may stop believing in your ability to reach that level of success.

Mistake #6 – You Lose Your Skills

If you are good at something, it's because you are skilled in it. To keep those skills, you have to nurture them. You shouldn't rely on what you have now or what you had in the past.

But when you become complacent, you stop improving. It gets worse as you may start losing the skills you once possessed. The ones that you enjoyed and could spend hours on may become not so enjoyable any longer. Unfortunately, your skills can slowly fade away if you stop nurturing them. If there's someone else around who hasn't stopped working on himself, you can easily lose your position to him.

Mistake #7 – You Stop Doing Things That Make You Happy

Not only can complacency make you stop nurturing your skills, but it can also prevent you from finding joy in the little things that used to bring satisfaction. Whether it is reading or going for a walk, your favourite past-times stop being so. Everything that requires effort is not so interesting to you anymore. Complacency is to blame for all of the above.

Why?

As you become resistant to change and as you lose your skills, connections, and habits, you also lose interest in things that made you happy.

In my keynotes I always say that progress does not mix with complacency

The single most important thing you can do if you want always to progress in life is avoid complacency. The more you settle for complacency, the more it ruins your life and dreams. It affects who you are and what you do in so many ways. You start losing connections, become lazier, start settling, and don't respond to change; that's only the beginning.

Although it may feel good sometimes, being stuck in your comfort zone is just going to push you further down. It'll soon become much harder to get back up.

That being said, here are 5 proven strategies that you can do immediately to keep on progressing your business, career, and your personal life.

Strategy #1. Recognising Complacency and Giving it Context

Vladimir Nabokov, the famed Russian-American author, understood the complex nature of complacency. He said, 'Complacency is a state of mind that exists only in retrospective: It has to be shattered before being ascertained.'

The one crucial thing when resolving any problem is acknowledging its existence. It's easy to slip into auto-mode without even noticing, especially after a streak of great results and achievements. Look at the daily routine in your business: Are you or your team taking a good situation for granted? Are you still doing everything that enabled you to achieve your goals?

As in all matters, context is vital. Perhaps you had a big win and didn't celebrate it properly. If so, make sure to recognise the success before moving forward and turn it into a challenge. Use your achievements as motivation and focus on the feeling of victory.

Strategy #2. Setting Goals and Having a Clear Purpose

Always having something new on the horizon is a great way to keep your business going. There should never be a long period between reaching one goal and setting the next one. New goals and challenges are what move us forward, give us the motivation, and inspire us to one-up what we've done so far.

However, people aren't machines. We need a clear purpose for most things we do to make our efforts worthwhile. Whatever your goals are, ensure there's an underlying reason why they matter and align those goals with your purpose.

Strategy #3. Importance of Competition

The modern world has a way of breeding complacency. Peter Thiel, the co-founder of PayPal, addressed that tendency in his quote: I do think there is this danger that our society has made its peace with decline. I'd like to jolt them out of their complacency a little bit.

Competition is a significant motivating factor for most people - whether it's against others or themselves. Naturally, to leverage competition for defeating complacency, it's essential to keep the competitive environment creative, constructive, and healthy.

Devise a way for your teams to surpass each other's results so that they become an inspiration to everyone. Alternatively, focus your energy on bettering a competitive business.

Strategy #4. Setting Unbreakable Commitments

Much of the force driving you forward starts with a decision. Although we tend to put too much stock in outside factors, everybody knows deep down that we choose how we'll interact with the world.

Setting and achieving goals is a decision as is not letting distractions hinder your progress; the same goes for becoming complacent. When you choose not to settle for past successes, growing content with where you are will become more challenging than pushing forward.

The commitment made to oneself, a group, or a company relies on setting high standards. It's imperative to keep your goals always on your mind and remain accountable and responsible for their fruition. Otherwise, complacency will find room to settle in.

Strategy #5. Creating a New Identity

Regarding, the intellectual force behind the American Civil Rights Movement, Benjamin Mays said, 'The tragedy of life is often not in our failure, but rather in our complacency.'

Success isn't the only cause of becoming complacent - failure can be that, too. Everybody fails sometimes, and some people can develop a defeatist mindset as a result. This is especially true following significant setbacks - you might feel as if where you're currently at is good enough and grow complacent due to a fear of failure.

The best way to react to such circumstances is by forgiving yourself and building your identity on perseverance. Don't think about yourself as the one that fails and makes mistakes - no one's immune to that. Instead, be the person who gets back on his feet. Push on, try again, and try the best you can - let that be the foundation of your new identity.

Final word

As humans, we strive to discover a purpose in everything we do, which is rarely staying in one place. While it's easy to let yourself forget what you're striving for and indulge in either the feeling of victory or defeat for too long, we're beings of inspiration, movement, and progress at our core.

Find your drive to remain successful or the necessary motivation to move on. Make that step in the right direction, and you will be ready to take on even the loftiest of goals.

You see no one is immune to complacency. Regardless of the level of success, complacency will creep in when you least expect.

If you want to gain more insights, you can book Dr. Hassan Younes to present at your event and take advantage of his proven strategies and methodologies that will lead you to greater improvement.

Dr. Hassan Younes

Hassanyounes.com

Dr. Hassan Younes Bio

Dr Hassan Younes is a keynote speaker, best-selling author, and a successful entrepreneur. Hassan has a background in aerospace engineering, business administration, organisational change, and business management across multiple diverse industries and over two decades in the education and training sector.

Throughout his professional career, Hassan has utilised his skills and experience in business management to build a successful vocational training organisation, multiple travel agencies, and an international education facility in the Philippines and has managed investment and property development projects. Hassan holds a Doctorate in Business Administration and an Honour's Degree in Aerospace Engineering from RMIT in Melbourne and other qualifications in Business Administration, Business Management, Accounting, and Education. As the Founder and CEO of the Training College of Australia, his passion is to raise the standards of early childhood educators and leaders in all business sectors.

Hassan is also the Founder and Chair of the International Academy of Marawi, Managing Director at Caradon Investments, Founder & Senior Business Coach for Lanao Business Services, and Managing Director at Arndell Park Early Childhood Learning Centre.

As an authority on Business Leadership, Business Management, and Education Skills Training and Entrepreneurship, Hassan is widely published Nationally and Internationally, providing valuable insights into the future of Leadership. Hassan works with businesses and business leaders to recognise key strategies for growth and success and to be aware of the pitfalls that are not always obvious yet can be devastating. Complacency is the silent killer of many successful business and can have disastrous outcomes. Hassan shares his knowledge and experience in captivating keynote presentations and workshops with powerful stories and strategies that transform business leaders and businesses.

Dr. Hassan Younes is the President of Professional Speakers Australia (PSA) for Victoria/Tasmania for 2021.

David Adams

Before You Know What's Next

By David Adams

Growing up, we didn't have a lot of money, but we had a lot of love. Dad taught me **work ethic and how to give time, talent, and treasure for the benefit of others**. I know this because every weekend was spent helping someone, somewhere, with something. Start time was always 5 a.m. Momma taught us to **study hard and play harder**. The play part was easy; however, we studied at the table together which must have been really frustrating for her. Teaching a dyslexic child such as I how to read and study was an impossible task! I grew up short, fat, and kind of cute. (Momma said so.) The bullying got so bad momma decided that I needed boxing lessons. I thought "What? You don't think I'm bleeding enough already?" I hated it! I'm a lover, not a fighter! She reluctantly let me out of it.

Mom was a Licensed Practical Nurse. She was wondering if she should go back to school as the hospital was eliminating the LPN position. Dad said, **"I have a really strong feeling that you need to further your education.** Something in my body just doesn't feel right." Mom went back to school, and after graduating as a Registered Nurse, anything that could go wrong with dad, did. **Preparing for what's next before you know what's next** saved the family finances, and I'm sure a few unsettling arguments!

Dad **sought out the world's leading expert** in the field of treating Dyslexia. I received the help needed for the synapses to connect efficiently. One problem I still had was at the age of thirteen I was still reading one...word...at...a...time. I was so frustrated. I wanted to run my head through a brick wall! My grades went from C's, D's, and F's to A's, B's and C's.

This same year my cousin J was trying to convince me to join the school wrestling team. I was in the middle of telling him "Hell No!" when his older brother stepped in. He was a large and very convincing active-duty Soldier for the US Army. He made my choice clear when he said "Davey (They called me Davey Crocket) you can either join the wrestling team, or my brothers and I are going to beat you up every day until you do!"

I said, "I think I'd like the wrestling team!" Freshman year, I was so bad that I lost my first five matches, and I wanted to quit.

Mom said, "What are you going to do about it?"

I said, "I just told you. I'm going to quit!"

She said "Quitting is not an option. Why don't you call your uncle Danny? He won Boxing's Feather Weight Championship of the World and held it for four years."

I called Danny and he said, "David, yes, I drank raw eggs and all the nutritional things one has to do, but more importantly **I was first in the gym, I was the last one to leave, and I worked harder and with more intensity than anyone else!"** When I showed up early, guess who was there? The state champions from the year before. When I started staying late, Coach was there working with us. The end of my senior season, I was favored to win the State Championship and just before we went to State, I broke my arm! The pains of 766 wasted hours of practice time shot through my arm and into my heart as I realized my Dream of winning a State Championship was over! After the team won the State Championship, I walked into the wrestling room standing alone staring at the names of all the State Champions from years past---the place I had imagined my name being every day for four years. I heard the door open, and Coach walked up, put his arm around my shoulders, and said "Davy, you are one of the greats!" I didn't fulfill my dream, but the lesson remained **"Show up early, stay late, work harder**

and more intensely than anyone else!"

I was such a good student by this time that I finally read my first book cover to cover my senior year. Yes, you know I skipped a few chapters just to turn the report in on time! After graduation a mentor called me into his office. He said, sliding a book across his desk, "You are going to read this book cover to cover over the next 90 days.

I replied, **"You know I am a dyslexic, right?"**

He said, "You have to be persistent and consistent."

I picked up the book and fanned the pages to the last one. "All 531 pages of it?"

He said, "Yes, all 531 pages of it!"

I took that book home, and I began to read. **I had made a commitment, and I knew I had to do it.** As I read, my eyes went blurry and then dark, followed by migraines. I continued to read, and 90 days later I was back into his office. Slamming the book down on his desk and shoving it towards him, I said, "I did it!!!!"

He said "That's great! Do it again in 30 days this time!"

I read that book again. Yes, all 531 pages of it and I continued to study for two hours per day for the next two years.

One day, I received a phone call "Hello!" It was my buddy Chris---you know, the friend who invites you to the "opportunity of a lifetime" meeting about once per week. "Chris, I told you I'm never going to another one of these meetings with you again!"

He said, "This one's in Vegas!"

I said, **"When do we leave?"**

We walked into the MGM Grand with 18,500 energetic people, singing, dancing, anticipating the arrival of the multi-millionaire Hubert Humphries. He was to lay out the strategies of how he made his fortune! Silence cleared the air as he approached the mic to speak. He said, "If I were you, I would take notes as if this is the last time you ever hear from me!"

Pen in hand I'm like "Give it to me, baby. Let's go!"

He said, "You need to do two things to be successful in life. Step one: go to Fantasy Island for 30 minutes every single day! Step two: read for 30 minutes every day, miss a meal, but never miss your thirty minutes of reading." I'm sure he borrowed that last line from Jim Rohn, but everything he said stabbed me deep in my heart. I was ashamed of myself. I hadn't read a book in years.

The day we got back home I bought a **stack of books to read.** Two of them changed my life. The first was Dig Your Well Before You're Thirsty by Harvey Mackay. Aside from being the best networking book ever written, it gave me this epiphany "David, if the highest paid people in the world are the best communicators. You, my friend, had better figure out how to communicate!" Jim Cathcart's book The Acorn Principle reinforced what Harvey taught me…when he quoted Earl Nightingale's late night radio show "If you will spend one extra hour each day studying in your chosen field, you will be a national expert in five years or less." They both recommended joining Toastmasters, and Jim joined the Jaycees. Both are communication and leadership training grounds. **I joined both!**

I was speaking in front of audiences for as long as I can remember. Momma or one of my sisters would whisper in my ear the words to parrot into the mic at Sunday school. I spoke often and yet without structure or real purpose. Joining these two organizations offered so much opportunity to conquer my insecurities and fears. They boosted my confidence and gave me a firm foundation from which to build!

I immediately entered Toastmasters' humorous speech contest after joining. I was so bad that no one laughed at my humorous speech for seven long minutes. Brutal! I entered another one, the "International Speech Contest". I placed third at the district level. After my presentation a man walked up to me and said, "How would you like to win this contest next year?"

I said, "Absolutely!"

Larry Lands became my first **speaking mentor,** an incredibly talented and gifted leader and communicator. He introduced me to Willy Jones, the 1997 World Champion of Public Speaking. With their leadership, hundreds of dollars invested in books, seminars, and other training, I invested in thousands of hours of writing, speaking, and practicing. On one occasion my buddy and I walked into an open mic night. I got up and spoke, and when I was finished, the emcee said, "Wow!!! That was the first "Attempt" at humor we have ever had in here!" That was the only laugh I heard that night. On other occasions my friend would gather random strangers off the street and ask them to listen to my presentation and give me feedback. I practiced in hundreds of Toastmasters clubs, Rotary, Lions, high schools, and elementary schools, and I even practiced in front of the homeless population at Waikiki Beach on Oahu. I won many Toastmasters speaking awards and the highest award the Jaycees give for speaking: "The 2004 Durward Howes Memorial Award in recognition as the outstanding speaker of The United States Junior Chamber". I have spoken to audiences from Hawaii to Florida for companies like Parsons Group, BNSF Railroad, Bank of Hawaii, Lee Container, CBC Bank, ACI, and numerous others. I tell you this not to impress you but to impress upon you that when you set out to learn something, when you put in the time, effort, and enthusiasm, and when you learn a skill to prepare for what's next, before you know what's next, good things happen!

In 2008, the United States Economy took a nosedive. My speaking mentors and I had started a business. The new economy killed it! We were making so much money that I had to lay myself off and move back to the mainland. I had to do something different. I felt lower than I had ever felt in my life, a complete failure. Desperate for a way to provide for my then wife and four children, I moved my family to Fort Worth, Texas. We moved into one bedroom of my brother-in-law's home.

I started working for one of the largest retailers in the world as an entry level overnight stocker making less money than I made mowing lawns at age of eleven. I had put on a few extra pounds and decided that I was going to let my new employer pay me to work out eight hours per day. I worked so hard and fast that they nicknamed me Speedy! On one occasion my direct supervisor came to me and said, **"Slow down. You're making us all look bad!"** Who knew that a little hustle could offend even a supervisor! I would sweat through four shirts per night and go home a sweaty mess. We only had one car, and on many occasions, I would walk the three miles home.

One day I noticed everyone walking to the front door. I asked a coworker what was going on, and she said, "It's break time." We all go outside for our break. I followed everyone outside.

I heard one man say, "This job sucks!"

I heard another say, "Our manager really is the worst!"

Then another "I got a line on a job down the road paying double what I'm making here!"

Then I heard the words of my father **"David, avoid negativity as if it were an infectious disease!"** I turned around and walked back into the building. I never took my break with those people again. Instead, **I sought out my managers** and peppered them with questions about the business, how it worked and the responsibilities, and how to get better.

I was on the job for two months when a position opened. I told my manager that I wanted an interview. He said, "You've only been here two months!"

I said, "Yes, and I would at least like an interview." Two weeks went by, and I asked him about the status.

He said, "Before the interview you were an unknown quantity. After the interview, I couldn't decide between you and the guy who had been here for five years. I asked my wife, my fellow manager, and even my boss. I have to go with the other guy."

I said lightheartedly, "That's ok. Everyone reserves the right to make the wrong decision once in a while."

Two weeks later I was promoted to a daytime management position for an additional $.10 an hour. What this promotion did is put me in proximity to the decision makers. In this meeting my manager said, "David, you can have, be, and do anything you want with this company! You just have to stake your flag and decide that this is what you are going to do! You have to go all in!"

I said, "Let's do it!" I went home and wrote at the top of my goals list Store Manager with a deadline of five years. I met the Store Director, the Marketing Director, and others whom I could learn from. My store manager was one of those leaders who always lifted his people up in front of his boss. He introduced me to the Market Manager, and I was able to find common interests by asking them questions about themselves. They took an interest in my development; they were in my corner. They all wanted to see me succeed. Now all I had to do was deliver. I started by teaching the people in my department how to do my job. Nine months later another position opened. **I asked for an interview.** My store director sent me an email that I still have today. He said, "That position is not equal to your skillset. Give me **90** more days, and I will make you a salaried manager in my building." True to his word, three months later he sent me to management school!

The amazing thing about being a salaried manager is that you don't have to take days off. You can arrive early and stay late, and you can work at high levels of intensity while you are there! This gave me the opportunity to shorten the learning curve. I started taking tough assignments and created a training program for middle managers. I was promoted again within the next year. I was shuffled around helping to clean up stores and build a new one from the ground up. That final promotion to store director came just two days before the "goal of five years" that I had set for myself.

I went from an $8 entry level position to a salaried position at over six figures in under five years. I left that company to pursue my purpose and to inspire leaders to embrace people stewardship so that their teams will take personal responsibility for their own growth and development.

Final Thoughts:

Gentlemen, the greatest take aways from my life so far are these…anything we want in life is attainable through

- Hard work, adding value and providing service to others. Always do more than you are currently being paid to do. The universe, God, whatever you believe in, will always reward you for it.

- We must determine what we want, what we want to give, and exactly why we want to give. How we give it comes naturally through your heart. Continue to clarify that vision every day. The question "How badly do you want it?" is answered by what you are willing to give in exchange for it? Then be consistent and persistent with daily action towards it. Remember, nothing substitutes for action. You cannot manifest it into your life without taking the required action.

- Avoid negativity as if it were an infectious disease. Turn off the TV; tune out the propaganda.

- Tune into positivity and that which will expand your minds vision. Read books, attend seminars, and listen to podcasts and all things that will positively alter the mind every day.

- Seek out positive mentors, teachers, visionaries, and network with them.

- Visualize your destination, your action steps to get there, the obstacles, and the workarounds and then take that next best action step. When you take an interest in yourself, others will take an interest in you. This is how the people who can help you will find you.

- Life is a balance of study hard, work hard, and play hard. As my mentor once told me "We all juggle a set of balls; some are glass some are plastic. Don't drop the glass ones." ---BG

- Prepare for what's next before you know what's next by developing the skills necessary for whatever your next level looks like.

- When you know what you want to learn or overcome, seek out the world's leading expert to help you learn or overcome the thing. Positive peer pressure is good when you know what you're being pressured to do is good for you. Surround yourself with people who will positively pressure you to stretch your vision, expand your skills, and accelerate your accomplishment.

- To attract the types of people into our lives that we want and need, we must work on becoming the kind of man that those people want in their lives. This includes those of you who are searching for the perfect partner. We must become the partner we are searching for---the version of the man that they will desire most.

- The only way to conquer your fears is to embrace them, dance with them, and utilize them to propel you through them and onto your next level of success.

Brothers, never quit! Never give up! Always be present! Always be positive!

Your past does not define you! The small shifts you make in your thinking, your actions, and your beliefs today will transform your tomorrow.

For more information on how to work with me directly for personal leadership coaching, keynote speaking, speaker training or help writing your own keynote speech, you can contact me directly at davidadamsspeaks.com or support@davidadamsspeaks.com.

Tommy Willis

Being a Man of Virtue

By Tommy Willis

Elder Tommy Willis married his first love in 2010, Evangelist Rosalind Willis-AKA Coach Roz. Between both, they have six children and thirteen grandchildren. He was ordained and licensed as an Elder in 2011. He has a bachelor's degree in General Studies with an emphasis in Religion. He has a master's degree in Addictions Counseling. He is a certified Christian life coach through BPMI Leadership and Life Coaching Institute Department of UGCS & UACCI Ministries. He is a published author. He and his wife have a publishing company called Birthing Books Publishing. The couple have been involved with Worldwide Voice in the Wilderness ministry going behind bars in the prisons and doing marriage ministry. They are volunteers for the state of Texas as marriage facilitators for a program called Twogether in Texas where couples getting married take an 8-hour course to get $65 off their marriage license. They also have their own marriage ministry where they counsel couples that are having problems or who are just looking for skills and tools to assist in their marriage. He also assists in cooking and assists any way he can for his wife as she has her Ladies Teas in the city for women in all walks of life. He is a member of the Alpha Phi Alpha Fraternity, Inc. since 1991. He was awarded the Black Blazer of Excellence & Achievements in 2021 and the GOHA (Gentlemen of Hearts Award) in 2021 for creative leadership and dedication.

Success to me is having obstacles and setbacks in your life and overcoming them. I believe that your past molds you for the man you are destined to be in the present. That's the good and the bad and sometimes the ugly. But it is up to us to learn from it, accept it, and grow from it. Also have faith and self-confidence in yourself and know that you are making a difference in other people's lives without expecting anything in return. Never compete with anyone but yourself. Be better than YOU. In other words, try to be better in every aspect of your life than you were the day before. Never cut corners and trust in your process because when God get you at the position, place, or title that you were destined to be, you will truly be proud of the progress you made knowing that you truly earned it.

One of my favorite poems I had the chance to learn while I was pledging into Alpha Phi Alpha Fraternity was the IF poem by Rudyard Kipling. At 20 years old I was just happy to memorize it and not let my Line Brothers down and be the reason we would get just a little more Wood on our back sides. I would like to share this poem with you.

If

If you can keep your head when all about you

Are losing theirs and blaming it on you,

If you can trust yourself when all men doubt you,

But make allowance for their doubting, too;

If you can wait and not be tired by waiting,

Or being lied about, don't deal in lies,

Or being hated, don't give way to hating,

And yet don't look too good, nor talk too wise:

If you can dream—and not make dreams your master;

If you can think—and not make thoughts your aim;

If you can meet with Triumph and Disaster

And treat those two impostors just the same;

If you can bear to hear the truth you've spoken

Twisted by knaves to make a trap for fools,

Or watch the things you gave your life to, broken,

And stoop and build 'em up with worn-out tools:

If you can make one heap of all your winnings
And risk it on one turn of pitch-and-toss,
And lose, and start again at your beginnings
And never breathe a word about your loss;
If you can force your heart and nerve and sinew
To serve your turn long after they are gone,
And so hold on when there is nothing in you
Except the Will which says to them: 'Hold on!'

If you can talk with crowds and keep your virtue,
Or walk with Kings—nor lose the common touch,
If neither foes nor loving friends can hurt you,
If all men count with you, but none too much;
If you can fill the unforgiving minute
With sixty seconds' worth of distance run,
Yours is the Earth and everything that's in it,
And—which is more—you'll be a Man, my son!

-Rudyard Kipling

Thirty years later from memorizing this poem and as I have gotten older and have been through some things in my life, now I understand what Mr. Kipling was trying to tell his only son John through this poem. You see he was providing him with instructions on how to become a man of virtue and in how to conduct himself with character and integrity in every situation that may come his way…from the good, the bad, and the ugly. Finally, he was giving him instructions in how to treat people from all walks of life in which we can learn from that in this day and age.

I read a book once by Stephen Covey called the 7 Habits of Highly Effective People. Habit 2 was to Begin with the End in Mind. He talks about how you would like something to turn out before you get started, so why not start with your life's walk. In how you treat people, set examples for others to follow on how to make a difference in their lives. In other words, when it is all said and done and everyone you encountered while you were on this earth had a chance to write the words on your tombstone, what would you want them to say about you? To me success is not how much money you have or the titles or credentials you have behind or in front of your name, but how you were able to use those titles and credentials to be of service to others.

To my younger generation: Always be true to yourself, believe in yourself, and never settle in life. Respect your elders and take a break from the X-boxes, Play Stations, and telephones, and if you are still blessed to have your grandparents, sit at their feet and gain a little wisdom while they are still with you. Be of service to others and above all else give God all the praises for every progress, accomplishments, setbacks, and comebacks. Never give up on your dreams-don't follow them-chase them. Always remember honesty, discipline, dedication, respect, loyalty, and integrity will assist you in being that man or woman that you were destined to be in this life! One of my favorite quotes is the following: What happens to a man is far less significant than what happens within a man. Trials and tribulations are going to come your way. That is all a part of life… how you deal with them is the defining answer. Whoever reads this may God bless you and keep you!

-     Tommy Willis

THE BLACK BLAZER

MEN ENTREPRENEURS "BLAZING TO SUCCESS"

Spencer Muldrow

THEY COUNTED ME OUT
By Spencer Muldrow

"Boy where did you get that roguish ass, devilish shit from?" One of my aunts asked me after bailing me out of jail at the age 12 for armed robbery. "We don't have any rogues in our family. We come from a long line of hard-working successful people; we ain't no damn crooks!" The only answer I could give her back then as I shamefully shrugged my shoulders and peered at the ground was "I don't know". Having spent over 14 years of my life behind bars in at least 12 different prisons and jails in four different states, I had plenty of time to pounder that question. I grew up in the 60's in government housing---the projects. I loved the projects and was quick to brag anywhere that I went "I from the old projects"!

I lived on the busiest street on the corner of a set of row houses. There were many families there with at least 5,6,7,8,9,10 kids per family; something was always going on. I could look out of my bedroom window and see all the older guys on the corner shooting dice, dressing in the latest clothes, driving nice cars, singing doo whoop to the latest songs---the Temptations, Four Tops, the Delfonics, Marvin Gay! I could sit on my back porch and look across the street at the biggest, busiest basketball court in the city and witness dealers selling drugs, smoking, and shooting drugs. I also had the privilege of watching and playing with some of the best basketball players that Virginia had to offer.

"Boy, where in the hell did you get that devilish ass roguish shit from?" I remember when I was four years old my siblings and I lived in a rat infested, dilapidated house built in the 1800's. The rats were big, bold, and aggressive! I still bear the scar on my left ear where a large rat attacked me while I was sleeping. It latched on to me like a pit bulldog and would not let go. But the most memorable event that happened in that house was when my mother put my three siblings and me to bed for our mid-day nap. While sleeping I was awakened to someone standing at the foot of my bed. I will never forget it!

I opened my eyes. There was a large, ugly, mean looking man peering at me! His eyebrows were squinched; he had a very large broad nose and small horns protruding from the top of his head. Taking very deep breaths, I could see his chest inhale and exhale. His nose would expand and deflate with each breath. Terrified, I attempted to scream and jump up, but I was stuck in my own body. I tried with every ounce of energy in my body to make a sound, to move my arms, my legs. It was as if I was glued to the bed. I have not experienced that degree of terror since that day.

He or should I say it was looking at me as if trying to decide what to do to me or with me. After what seemed like an hour, it just dissipated down into the floor. Then I could move. I remember quietly getting out of the bed, being careful not to wake my brother who was a year older than me sleeping in the bed next to mine. I was four years old. This was 1962........Cowboys and Indians was our favorite game to play. My mother brought us cowboy boots, leather gun holsters, and metal cap guns that fit in the holsters. In my underwear I put on my cowboy boots and strapped on my gun holster and quietly crept downstairs, went out into the back yard, and started chasing the four little chicks my mother had brought for my three siblings and me for the upcoming Easter holiday.

The next thing I knew I struck one of them across the head with the butt of the gun rendering it immobile. As it flailed around on the ground, I continued to strike it in the head until it stopped moving. I continued this process with the other three chicks until all four chicks were dead. It was as if I was in some sort of trance. I will never forget the look on my mother's face when she opened the back door. Her eyes and mouth opened very widely; she then put her hand over her mouth. She screamed my name out "Spencer.......OH MY GOD!" She ran over to me, kneeled, and hugged me tightly while repeating "FATHER…... FATHER…...OH MY GOD……. OH, FATHER."

I started the first grade at Charles Huston Elementary at the age of six. I never attended a pre-K or kindergarten. I was never prepped for first grade. I had not learned my alphabets or learned basic sight words or basic addition like 2+2 or 3+3, things of that nature. So school was a real challenge for me. I could not understand why most of the kids knew how to read books like Dick and Jane, and I did not. There were a few other classmates who appeared to be in the same boat as I was.

Right from the start I stayed in trouble for one thing or another. By the third grade I was fighting kids and teachers. I am sure I got suspended more times than anyone during my tenure at Charles Huston Elementary. While in the six grade I got in a fight during recess. My teacher, the only white teacher, grabbed my arm to take me to the principal's office. I struggled with her and broke away. She continued to walk to the school, looking back at me scolding me. A trash truck backing up from the trash furnace hit her in the head! The janitor Mr. Brooks ran over and picked her up. I got suspended for that.

"Boy, where in the hell you get that devilish shit from?" By the time I hit seventh grade I was the leader who first committed some serious crimes---car thefts, home and business burglaries, robbing people, shooting dice, purse snatching. During the day or nighttime, we would go out in crews. Everyone wanted to travel with me because I was ruthless and would not come back to the hood empty handed. "Boy, Boy, Boy, where in the hell did you get that devilish shit from?"

If I could have looked out of my windows and could have seen more doctors, lawyers, and businessmen type dudes…who knows maybe they would have had a greater influence on my future aspirations, but I took a certain pride and pleasure in being known as a hustling ass young boy. I used to break in clothing stores in Old Town Alexandria. By the time I got to the ninth grade I had been involved in some renowned break ins and stick ups and was darn proud of it.

In 1975 I started the tenth grade. My brother was a wrestler, so I joined the wrestling team. I was pretty good at it until I got put off the team for being too aggressive. One night in October I was standing on the block. One of the older neighborhood hustlers drove up in his "Duce and A Quarter" and told me he had a hit. I proudly got in the car. We drove off, picked up another older cat across town, and committed a home invasion in the Landmark area of Alexandria, VA.

Things went sour right from the start! A teenage girl in the apartment knew me! There was no money found in the apartment, only a large amount of PCP, ACID, and other PSYCHEDELIC type drugs. I was soon caught in December. I was sentenced to three years in the state penitentiary. I will never forget my mother in the court room crying and begging the judge telling him "It's not fair. It's just not fair!"

The judge responded, "Ms. Muldrow, what do you want us to do? We can not just let him go because he is going to get hurt. Someone is going to kill him at the rate he is going. It is the opinion of the courts that he is no more than a hoodlum, a thug, and a gangster!"

In some strange way, I was proud of my validated title. After all that is what I aspired to be. "Boy, Boy, Boy, where in the hell did you get that devilish ass shit from?" At sixteen, I was the youngest inmate there, so I always had a point to prove. I witnessed a lot of violence by inmates and guards. I stayed in trouble for one thing or another. I was placed in solitary confinement on many occasions for violence towards other inmates and mostly refusing to work. Once while out on the chain gang in the back woods of Chesterfield, VA, on a lunch break all of us inmates were talking about what we were going to do once we got out. Some exclaimed that they would be hustlers for life. I exclaimed "Mannnnnn....... I'm ma try to stop as many people as I can from going through this bullshit. This shit is slavery! Man......I'm gonna work at a juvenile detention center when I get out of here.

That's when one of the guards with a wide brim hat on his head with mirrored sunglasses, sitting on top of a real tall horse yelled out....... "Aww Muldrow. you ain't shit and you will never be shit! Now stop all that jaw jappen and pick up that jack hammer and get back to work." That statement felt as if someone had hit me with a jolt of electricity. Those words really hurt me and have haunted me throughout my entire life! I had to prove him wrong. Once while I was in solitary confinement "The Hole" for refusing to work, one of the trustees delivered my breakfast tray. I told him I would be willing to try anything to get out off the chain gang. So, he managed to talk to the right people, and I got a job in the prison bakery. I learned to bake cakes, pies, cookies, loaf bread, biscuits, doughnuts. I became pretty good at it and took a lot of pride in watching all the inmates eating my finished products. This was the only positive thing I learned to do while I was there. The prison had no educational programs. I went in without a high school diploma, and I came out without one, but I did learn how to be a better dice and card cheater. My reading and writing were probably on a six-grade level. I was released in September 1978.

Once back in Alexandria, I saw that much had not really changed. Most of the people I ran with were doing the same thing or in some prison or jail. One of my hustling buddies had even gotten killed. Another hustling buddy had joined the military. I quickly realized the streets had nothing to offer me. Jasper went to the military and that really did not sound like the worst idea in the world; at least it would get me away from Alexandria, VA. Plus, I was in pretty good shape from working on the chain gang.

I remember proudly walking into the recruitment office on Washington Street ready to be signed up and saying to myself I'm getting away from this place. I am going to do something different with my life......I'm going to make my momma proud of me! The interview with the recruiter lasted about five minutes. He informed me I was an ex-convict, did not have a high school diploma, and did not qualify! I'll never forget that feeling of not feeling good enough! On my long walk home, I even went into a few business establishments seeking employment. Each one rejected me for the same reasons. After a few more days of going out looking for a job, something evil inside of me started speaking, "You see, MoJoe, you out here trying to do the right thing, but these motherfuckers just won't let you! I bet if you put that gun in your hand, they will give you some respect then!"

Foolishly, my brother and I had robbed a bank for twenty-five thousand dollars. Instead of the money making my life easier, it made my life a living hell. I had to constantly look over my shoulders for the FBI and the niggas on the streets. My mom's house was burglarized and ransacked; a molly cocktail was thrown through our window; there was an attempt to kidnap my brother and collect a ransom. The ironic thing is I got a job at a silk screen printing company a week after robbing the bank and worked there for about five months. One day while working the printing press, someone tapped me on my shoulder. It was a white man in a suit with a shiny badge, "Spencer Muldrow, special agent such and such with the FBI, you are under arrest for bank robbery." I was escorted out of the building to the glare of news cameras and reporters.

Across town my brother was being arrested and experiencing the exact same thing. We were on the 5'oclock news. I felt so bad for him and my mother. This was all my fault. They sent my brother to a federal prison in Morgantown, WV. They sent me to a maximum-security prison in Petersburg, VA. My first day there I witnessed a guy being chased down and stabbed. It was a renegade survival of the fittest type of environment. I was eighteen and in the major league now! I was tested on a couple of occasions, and I knew all eyes were on me to see how I responded. I had to respond violently to all challenges and tests.

Soon I found myself in the hole for breaking a pool stick across a Mexican dude's head. They would not allow me to come out because they claimed there was a Mexican contract on my life. After being in the hole for about six months, they came to my cell early one morning and put chains around my ankles, waist, and wrist. They drove me to Richmond, VA, airport, put me on an airplane with federal agents, and flew me to the Butner Federal Reformatory in Butner, NC. "Boy, where in the hell did you get that devilish shit from?" That prison was more laid back and built for high-profile white-collar type prisoners. It is the same place they sent Jim Baker, John Hinkley, Mayor Marion Berry, John DeLorean, and Bernie Madoff.

At Butner I enrolled in the GED program and achieved it in five months. That accomplishment encouraged me to enroll in some college courses such as self-image psychology, sociology, business law, public speaking, and anything else I felt might put more strength in my struggle to be "Shit in Life". I was still the youngest inmate there, but the older dudes were better role models. There was very little need to wear my tough guy hat there. We did a lot of studying and testing each other's wits.

I accomplished a few certificates of achievements and was released in 1980---ready for the world. I had goals firmly planted in my brain. I wanted to work at a juvenile detention center. I learned to lay brick while there, so I got a job laying brick. Mannnnn......now that is some hot hard work! But I stuck it out for about six months. Then one day on the job the boss's son called me a stupid ass nigger. Before I knew it, I had punched him in the face, and we got into a knock down drag out brawl. That was my last day on that job.

I looked at my goals hanging on the refrigerator. Goal 3 "Get a job at the same Juvenile detention center I was locked up in as a kid." I went out to the Alexandria Juvenile Detention Center in Landmark and made them aware of my goals. Surprisingly receptive to me, the man stated they had no counselor openings. But there was a brand-new juvenile facility set to open soon in Fairfax County, VA. He made a call to the director and told him he had someone he thought he should meet. I drove over, met the director, and expressed my passion to work with at risk kids and be a positive motivating force. After an hour interview, I was informed there were no counselor positions. Noticing I had my baking certificate, he asked if I knew how to bake well enough to teach it. I was hired as an assistant food service manager and baking instructor. Three years later I received an outstanding performance award for dedicated service.

One day I was shopping at a Safeway Supermarket. As I walked through the bakery, a young lady began screaming, ran from behind the counter, began hugging me, and yelling, "Oh my God, this is the man that changed my life. This is the man that taught me to bake when I was in that juvenile place!" I remembered her because she suffered from explosive personality disorder but did well in my class. I was so proud I had touched her life and helped her to believe that other people's thoughts about her did not define her or what God ultimately had in store for her.

I have proven that prison guard up on that horse wrong! Today

I have a beautiful wife, thirteen grandchildren, a beautiful home, every materialistic possession that I desire, and enough to give away---nothing as a result of ill-gotten gain. I have rebuked that ugly man that came in my room when I was four years old. I have given my life to God; He orders my steps now! OH...... by the way, did I mention that I was recently presented with an Honorary Doctorate Degree in Humanitarianism! And have been given a full pardon from the governor of VA. Ain't God Good!

Over the past twenty years I've managed group homes for troubled and abused youth. I worked as a counselor, art teacher, life coach, gym director, and basketball coach. I like to tell my story to young people more because that's who I feel can benefit from it the most.

Mikey Adam Cohen

Invest in the Present. Change the Future
By Mikey Adam Cohen

I Made My Bed This Morning! The Secret Sauce to Transform into A Leadership Boss! Human Soul Ontological Mentoring Inside I Got Out of My Own Way…You can, too…Hold Tight!!! Your life is about to blast into the stratosphere. 10, 9, 8, 7, 6, 5, 4, 3, 2, 1!

The universe wants you to thrive. It wants to support you in that thriving. Because if you're thriving in your well-being and in your magic, that means you can support other humans to do the same. That only helps expand the collective consciousness of humanity---you glowing and doing and living well is of the highest service to the universe.

This is why the principles of manifesting with the law of attraction are sound and simple. It only takes for you to shift your thoughts and feelings from a place of lack to a place of having. That was the missing piece for me. Though I had read many times that when you focus on lack, you only attract more of it, I didn't quite grasp the profundity of that statement. I would journal and affirm and pray daily for my desires to manifest, and nothing would happen. Reshape the way you think about progress and success and find the tools and strategies you need to transform your habits—whether you are a team looking to win a championship, an organization hoping to redefine an industry, or simply an individual who wishes to quit smoking, lose weight, reduce stress, and achieve success that lasts. Most Influential People and Most Influential Kids Surrounded by Greatness Nonprofit was started by humble magic.

Mikey is a dad of a cute little special French Bulldog named Little! Mikey often brings his puppy to many of his high-profile board meetings. He is also a son to two extraordinary parents, a brother to two younger brilliant other boys, a fantastic friend to everyone, and an activist that loves to serve make a difference. A global backstage music and entertainment photographer / writer / behind-the-scenes music festival entertainment reporter, motivational coach, and strategist with huge attention to detail with his sold-out motivational conferences and custom music events, Mikey Adam Cohen began a decade of mindfulness practices after a dear friend that's an icon in the music business Peter White told him his approach wasn't in-kind to get the project done! Without knowing he took immediate responsibility, and this has helped him breathe during difficult emotions before becoming anxious, overcoming his self-doubt, and often spiral.

These last couple of years have been incredibly significant after one of Mikey's dear friends and mentors gave him the tools needed to separate the emotions in intelligent response from the part that has grown beyond its useful life and become excessive and destructive. His passion is helping others showcase their brand, connecting them with who they need to be successful! Motivational Icon Harrison Klein is Mikey Adam Cohen's go-to expert. He helped him to get out of his own way and begin to manifest and build the life he had always dreamed of having. Mikey is ready to share his lifelong knowledge and his secrets---that secret sauce to a big boss! In an uncertainty in the world such as the pandemic, the economy, and circumstances beyond your control, changing and manifesting a new reality is relatively simple to take action and learn. Take notice to ride the wave of discomfort; this is the point at which momentum is sparked and often leads you to realize the life you deserve! Now you can Identify the next best steps and how to spot those sneaky (but attractive) false paths that can keep you living small. It's time to play big! You were born to win! Invest in the Present.! So, with the ability to mindread he became a master Connector and has worked with and collaborated and partnered with some of the biggest people in the world! He is always excited to collaborate...

Change the Future

Did you know that your goals, dreams, and aspirations are real? They are important, and they are achievable. Young people do not need fixing; they need champions who see them for who they really are and who they can become. Every young person possesses the potential to become a community leader and should have the opportunity to reach their full potential. Mikey Adam Cohen inspires kids to discover their purpose and showcase it with others helping them step into greatness so they can raise their vibration and inspire action takers that can be mentored into the leaders of tomorrow and return the favor! You could say he's always been passionate about the power of leadership, a big believer in creating a collaborative consciousness to help kids discover their purpose and then hone into their emotional intelligence, well-being, and peak performance in order for us to create together a peak potential leadership culture. He's always been passionate about the power of mentoring,

Mikey Adam Cohen is the behind the scenes driving force behind sold out motivational summits, connecting the right people with the right talent to accomplish their goals as a master connector with a roster of millions of contacts the best in the business! He has inspired youth to stretch, pushed them beyond their limits in spite of their fears and doubt. His story of grit, perseverance, courage, and growth through change has motivated the masses to overcome their challenges and boost morale. He reminds his listeners that success is about having mindful resilience, flexibility, and personal accountability. Mikey's journey to wellness began when he was born with a rare, yet severe genetic disease called XYY Marfans Syndrome which he has been disabled with for his lifetime but through personal development from his mentors has beat the odds and is thriving and helping others do the same.

Mikey defied logic, beat the odds, and snatched victory out of the jaw of adversity

Mikey Adam Cohen's journey started when he was born. "I came to understand that the reason why my affirming and journaling could not get any traction or momentum was because I was engaging my heart and mind in the vibration of lack. I was focusing my energy on what it felt like to not have those things---what it felt like to not have money--- what it felt like to not feel worth---what it felt like to not feel loved. So, the universe kept giving me more and more and more of that focused energy. That's because there's an unlimited, unfathomable amount of energy, and source that just wants to give you more and more of it because it does not want you to ever lack. You are so worth it."

"So, join me and become a vibrational match to the things you want: Match Your Vibration with Your Desired Reality."

"Remember you must approach these practices from a mindset of overflow. Okay, let's get to it. Harness that Power to partner with the energy of the Universe to accomplish your goals and dreams---the power to expand and express your creativity and consciousness without sacrificing your daily responsibilities to showcase to you great trainings, quantum healings, and big blessings daily. I live to serve! In this story, I'll be sharing with you an incredibly and highly effective way to become a vibrational alignment to the things you're wishing to manifest into your physical reality. When I first ventured on my conscious manifesting journey, I had no clue on what I was doing. I took the NLP certification class and was more aligned with my inner self and started speaking on as many stages as I could. This year I gave keynotes on the following: Allowing myself to be happy and full when the universe and my family say different. Hate As a Defense Mechanism, Reciprocity, and Consistency!"

"Trust me I was born a genetically disabled Keyota Empath.

Everyone has a dream goal if not many...It's time you actualized them. If you have big goals and an entrepreneurial mindset, this will radically expand what you're capable of achieving in life. Let me help you trigger flow states consistently so you can spend all day in that hyper productive zone. As long as I can remember, I've been a leader! Yet I've struggled with distraction, self- sabotage , and uncertainty. Are you ready to spend your entire workday in that hyper focused zone and say goodbye to the distractions of politics, colleagues, and trivial nonsense? Let's Remove All Self-Sabotage, Urgency, And Overwhelm so that you can be fully present with your family and those who matter to you."

Surrendering To Your Biology

It's time to dig deep into your belief system and uncover what's holding you back. You are about to leave with a plan for your LIFE and a strategy for its implementation. It's time to improve your life. Do your best to have the most rewarding experience. The first thing that will change everything in your life is to take full responsibility for everything in your life! Thanks, will come back later. Also, be more attentive. Make it your daily practice! But what does this actually mean? When we are mindful, we bring our full consciousness, awareness of what we are currently experiencing, to the fore. This is all we see, hear, think and feel. It sounds like you know a lot, but recently I've been spending quite a bit of time thinking about this idea and realized that we humans spend way too much time in constant overload. We always rush the day and clear the box from the list. It's more normal to say "I don't have time" when told to slow down and relax. 'It's not a shopping cart; it's a pause that actually exists. But the fact is that it really matters a lot when we realize its importance and put our intentional practice into practice.

"When you are given the opportunity to lead and they are developed as a leader, amazing things happen! I know this from experience during my role on working on and attending San Diego City Hall meetings with Mayor Maureen O'Connor's Mayor's Youth Summit that young people have been the driving force in raising millions to help our partner organizations combat some of the world's most pressing issues. My biggest setback was... my inner critic. For the longest time I rarely gave myself credit for my accomplishments. I thought that any success I achieved was a result of luck or external forces outside of my control. My inner critic produced a lot of self-doubt, feelings of inadequacy, and caused me to fall into negative thinking traps. I overcame it by... meditating and practicing mindfulness, being more kind to myself, and being vulnerable by talking about my inner critic. Sometimes I still doubt my abilities; however, placing more emphasis on what I do rather than what I get from what I do has helped increase my happiness and gratitude. Bringing people's voices and perspectives to the forefront helps humanize their experiences and creates unity among diversity."

These "Quantum Powers" are inactive in most of us, but Mikey has figured out how to activate them, so...If you aren't familiar with Mikey Adam Cohen, he's an internationally renowned influencer, one of the worlds most trusted/favored influencer/master connectors/on purpose creatives! When he was just a teenager sitting on the San Diego City council as a part of the mayor's youth summit, Cohen has worked as a backstage and onset entertainment reporter at the biggest musical festivals and award shows in existence! It was during that process that Cohen's icon, Al Jareau, gave Cohen the name "Mr Bigstuff, the single most important person alive instilling mindful human potential into his everyday existence!" said Al Jareau.

Vibration is thought + feeling = emotion. When you think genuinely about a certain thought, you experience a certain feeling about the thing that you're pondering on. In other words, how you feel about a certain thing is your vibration, and that is the secret to manifesting, for you to attract your desire you need to consistently let go of a lot in order to raise the frequency of your vibration, so you can manifest your desire. The universe wants you to thrive. It wants to support you in that thriving. Because if you're thriving in your well-being and in your magic, that means you can support other humans to do the same. And that only helps expand the collective consciousness of humanity. You glowing and doing and living well are of the highest service to the universe. This is why the principles of manifesting with the law of attraction are sound and simple.

"It only takes for you to shift your thoughts and feelings from a place of lack to a place of having. That was the missing piece for me. Though I had read many times that when you focus on lack, you only attract more of it, I didn't quite grasp the profundity of that statement. I would journal and affirm and pray daily for my desires to manifest, and nothing would happen. You need to reshape the way you think about progress and success and get the tools and strategies you need to transform your habits. As I began to understand that the reason why my affirming and journaling could not get any traction or momentum was because I was engaging my heart and mind in the vibration of lack. I was focusing my energy on what it felt like to not have those things. What it felt like to not have money. What it felt like to not feel worthy. What it felt like to not feel loved. So the universe kept giving me more and more and more of that focused energy. And that's because there's an unlimited, unfathomable amount of energy and God just wants to give you more and more of it because it does not want you to ever lack. You are so worthy."

"Here is my #1 way to become a vibrational match to the things I'm wanting."

Matching Your Vibration with Your Desired Reality.

"Remember you must approach these practices from a mindset

of overflow. Okay, let's get to it The Power of Music for Instant Vibrational Alignment. I was born a Keyota Empath with a severely disabling mental disability that challenged me for a good 90% of his life until I got trained by the most Influential people in existence to get out of my own way; it's our responsibility to close equity gaps and foster a culture of inclusion and equality. I mentor kids in leading with Empathy, Transparency, and Vulnerability. I like to create heart centered, mindful leaders that cultivate trust and full engagement with the joy of listening and acknowledgment of one another, to be a champion like myself of diversity in a purpose-driven culture that produces results in order to thrive! During this uncertain time join me in creating a more collaborate culture built on trust where full engagement thrives. I have been some of the world's most trusted pro-bono advisors working with the most influential entertainers, actors, motivational speakers, teachers, philanthropists, and CEOs of our generation. I'm so passionate about their purpose and inspired by why they do what they do. My work is in music/entertainment media team and relationships management, executive presence, psychological safety, resilience under pressure, team leadership, and developing empathy and compassion in a backstage music festival chaotic environment."

"With that being said, I encourage you to disrupt your paradigm and put a dent in systemic racism in our global culture. It's in our schools, churches, and the workforce. We seek to break down the barriers rooted in prejudices and biases and educate people. They shouldn't predetermine one's character based on the color of your skin. I remind my followers that success is about having mindful resilience, flexibility, and personal accountability. Excuses and justifications are dream killers. We all have the power to choose how we respond to external circumstances. Did you know that fostering leadership can be a lifelong process? I'm constantly growing and developing. I want you to see everything from the perspective of others. Good communication is an important factor in becoming an effective leader. Remember to listen carefully and treat others calmly and with respect. I had to build my confidence, and then there was nothing that prevented me from doing it. It's a big job to make sure all your classmates are playing their part."

"I recommend that you make the following small decisions: Which activity do you want to participate in? Rome wasn't built in a day! When I was a kid, I felt overwhelmed, so I avoided managerial positions. Create lists and divide your needs into viable ways to achieve them. I advise you not to be afraid of being different or pursuing what you are interested in. Go with your instinct; it won't lead you in the wrong direction ... read as many books as you can! Why do you ask? You will be all the experts you read, and your words will be your greatest strength."

"My advice for young professionals is to look at failures as learning opportunities, be vulnerable, and do not take no for an answer! As youth, we are sometimes underestimated because we are viewed as being "too young" or "lacking in experience." As the next generation of change-makers, our responsibility is to collaborate with others and advocate for our passions. We deserve to have our voices be heard! My best advice from a mentor was... to remember that whenever I am feeling uncertain or overwhelmed, I need to keep in mind the following mantras: "This too shall pass!" "Am I being the best version of me?"

"My biggest setback was... my inner critic. For the longest time I rarely gave myself credit for my accomplishments. I thought that any success I achieved was a result of luck or external forces outside of my control. My inner critic produced a lot of self-doubt and feelings of inadequacy and caused me to fall into negative thinking traps. I overcame it by... meditating and practicing mindfulness, being more kind to myself, and being vulnerable by talking about my inner critic. Sometimes I still doubt my abilities; however, placing more emphasis on what I do rather than what I get from what I do, has helped increase my happiness and gratitude."

"I have been told my whole life that I didn't do things correctly. These negative comments had a profound effect on my self confidence and self-esteem. Even if I gave everything, it wasn't enough. These comments had a huge impact on my self-confidence and self- esteem. I have some additional words of wisdom for tomorrow's hearty and essentially motivated leader ... You have the power to step into greatness and create epic memories in your life. If ever you are not satisfied, you can get out of the old paradigm!"

"Tomorrow is a new day! You may free yourself from misunderstandings and family dramas! I'm this living example ... I wish I had been taught the infinite freedom of expression--- freedom of sight! Freedom of action! You are free to express yourself in every aspect of your life. Anything is possible once you find your purpose. You are free to complete your higher missions! You can also receive a wealth of things just to be yourself. So, I learned one or two things to lift and step my vibrations! Now I am ready to strengthen you! I want you to be able to carefully magnetize your best life, fulfill your mission, and spread your message and shine like the light guide you are! You are all born leaders."

Contact Mikey if you need his help.

Mikey Adam Cohen 619-788-4291

Most Influential Kids Surrounded by Greatness

MostInfluentialMikey@gmail.com

Please Follow me @paradigmdisruptor

Photo Credit Ann Landstrom

Brandon Pillay

The People's Champion from Humble Beginnings

By Brandon Pillay

When I think back over my life, it almost seems like a blur. It seems almost yesterday that I was a child in my mother's arms. It seems like a moment ago that my father took me to school for the very first time. I grew up in a large family whose parents had even bigger hearts. There were many mouths to feed, but my mother never turned a neighbour's child away or an uncle who had fallen on hard times.

Growing up in a large family has its plusses. You never feel alone. You feel protected and loved although it has its shortcomings. But it teaches you to share, to make compromises, and to know your place.

I think one of the seminal influences was growing up in Unit Two, Chatsworth, which later came to be known as Bayview. No matter what apartheid had thrown at us, we had a sense of survival and community. We had our gangs, drug wars, and poverty. But we also had each other.

Sometimes it takes a moment to change your life and set it on a journey you never envisaged. This is what happened to me. In 1998 Fatima Meer came to Unit Two. It was a time of electricity cut offs and evictions, and this lady inspired me. She had been to jail, banned, and was a professor, but she was so humble. I became a civic activist and a leader of the Bayview Flat Residents Association (BFRA). It was a whirlwind as I marched with people, negotiated, fought street battles. In a short time, I turned from a young boy into a man who took responsibility.

I started working at the tender age of 12. Whilst some may think it is child labour, I saw it as being responsible and independent.

Although it was menial tasks at that age, it was still a job as I was remunerated for it. I started off as a paper boy delivering the paper within my community after school and on weekends. I continued with this job until the middle of high school when I then started working at Bedding and Linen shop, the famous GH Seedat in Clairwood, still being in school and my first attempts at taking public transport. It wasn't too difficult or scary as a few young people from my neighbourhood were working there as well. These were motivated young people who didn't drop out of school and made education their priority but worked on the holidays especially during the December period just so that they could do Christmas shopping.

Having grown up in a predominantly underprivileged community, we all knew how difficult life was and did not want to burden our parents further to do our shopping. This taught us all independence from an early age but more especially exposed us to the working environment. I went on to do other piece meal work until I finished matric. Again, circumstances did not allow me to further my studies, so I joined a Christian Organisation Scripture Union and taught life skills at primary and secondary schools receiving a stipend of R500 a month for almost 3 years. I never touched a single cent from it and gave the entire amount to my mum; that was the least I could do for the many years of sacrifice she made. I have counselled and mentored young people in the community and rehabilitated many young people who were on the drugs. I still didn't give up. I persisted. and then my life turned around when I started working as a full-time volunteer in my community of Bayview.

I started my real job out of school based at the University of Kwazulu Natal, Prof. Meers Institute for Black Research. While working here I met the one person who has had the greatest influence on my life Mr. Ramesh Harcharan. This is where I had a fledge for politics and learnt so much about our history. I did not have the finances to study and through my volunteering and after meeting Prof Ashwin Desai, he introduced me to another remarkable human being Saranel Benjamin who at the time was working at the Workers College. I secured a bursary to complete my first qualification, a diploma in Community development and political science. This was my first formal studies after matric, and I remember graduating with my mum and sister at my side with a special award for being the top student in the class.

In the year 1999 I was introduced to the Umptap Centre in Durban and attended a one-week course on Peace and Anti Racism Education. This was another turning point in my life, and I became an advocate for Peace and Anti Racism. I believe that we all belong to one race which is the Human Race. I have worked with the Umtapo Centre and have established peace clubs and peace forums within schools and communities as well as launched and ran many youth clubs. I continued my relationship and networking with the Umtapo Centre, and in 2001 I was selected as one of 15 young people from across the country to be part of a fellowship programme in the Netherlands. This programme was made possible through the Netherlands Embassy and RADAR a sister organisation to Umtapo that is based in Rotterdam. We attended classes at the Ichtuus University and visited RADAR, sadly my stay in Holland which should have been for one month was cut short as I became home sick and started experiencing anxiety attacks, I had to take a flight back home before completing the programme. After many years I had another amazing opportunity which was made possible through Umtapo Centre. I was selected with another peace activist Madoda to attend a Summer School for International Activists in South Wales at the St Donats Castle. We were only two young people from South Africa. We had the opportunity to interact with young people from all over the world.

I was one who always encouraged young people to work even if it was voluntary as they were able to gain work experience. I had the opportunity of meeting one of the greatest statesmen to ever walk this earth, former State President Nelson Mandela when he came to Chatsworth to meet the families of the Throb nightclub disaster; later he pledged to build a youth centre. Today we have the Chatsworth Youth centre. I played an instrumental role in the design and set up of the centre.

I was the founder and president of the Chatsworth Youth League after the Throb disaster. The league brought together young people from all walks of life in Chatsworth. I later also became the president of the Chatsworth Youth Forum based at the child welfare which became an umbrella body of youth groups. I have always had a passion for young people and started my activism from high school when I served many social clubs, SRS, and later the RCL.

I ensured that all through my life I continued to work. I worked with many projects and programmes for short periods until I secured a permanent job in the municipality as a programme officer. I was responsible for a large budget that dealt with setting up community projects called community-based planning. As the co-ordinator/ programme officer for CBP, I also started and headed the ID Campaign; later it became the National Population Registration Campaign (NPRC). As eThekwini Municipality we ran one of the most successful ID projects, and I had the opportunity to be invited by the then Minister of Home Affairs, Dr Nksosazana Dlamini Zuma to attend the portfolio committee on Home Affairs meeting in Parliament and later visited one of the recently converted smart home affairs offices in Cape Town. My 6 years at the municipality were the most fulfilling as every task that was executed was creating a better life for citizens in the city.

At the age of 30, actually on my 30th birthday, the 18th of May 2011, I was elected Ward Councillor for Ward 69 in Chatsworth. This was the first time that the ANC ever won this ward. Ward 69 was unique as for the first time after the ward demarcations and delimitations a portion of Lamontville was demarcated to Chatsworth and included into ward 69, this meant that the ward had both an Indian and African township as one ward. It was challenging but exciting to be able to work with a diverse community. Serving as a ward councillor kept me close to my roots and the ideals that motivated me in the first place.

Every day when I come home to my community I think about my parents and hope they are proud of me. I think about the opportunities I have had and hope I have made just use of them, not only for myself but for my community.

My job as a councillor was very demanding but at the end of the day, I felt fulfilment just as long as I am able to make someone else happy and have a smile as they go to bed. My motto in life is to never give up, and I take the words of our icon Tata Madiba "It always seems impossible until it is done." My strong biblical principles teach me that if a man does not work, he should not eat. We must, no matter how hard it is, make every effort to work or find work.

I think about the young people of my area and pray and hope that they will also have a moment as I did in 1998 that changed my life for the better.

I started many community projects and created many links and built networks. One such project was ladies who got involved in the saris for good karma project, they were donated sewing machines by SAB and know run their own small home businesses making money out of sewing.

I have facilitated many training courses and workshops at no cost to the community, by networking with other organisations NGO; s and government. One such accolade is the participants who underwent HIV AIDS training and TB dots, many of them have now become stipended Community Care Givers CCG's.

Through my community work with the BFRA we later established the Ubuntu Community Development and started work on Gender based violence within the community, we formed a partnership with the Foundation for Professional Development and had all our volunteers trained and empowered, I was successful in receiving a full scholarship through FPD and Yale University to complete a one-year programme on Advanced Health Management, I graduated here with Cum Laude.

In 2016 I contested the local government elections again, however, I did not emerge and used the time register for my honour's degree. I went on to complete a Bachelor of Public Administration Honours at MANCOSA and successfully graduated. In 2018 I took up a full-time position within eThekwini Municipality, Community Participation Unit, as a Manager for the Grant in Aid Office. This was by far the best experience ever and the job that I enjoyed most. My office was responsible for providing funding to Non-profit Organisations within the city to enhance their work or run special projects. The other component was to provide capacity building in the form of trainings and workshops. In January 2021 I was sworn in as a member of parliament in the National Assembly---Parliament of RSA. This announcement came in the midst of the storm. On the 25th of December 2020 (Christmas day) my entire family was infected with COVID; this was the Delta variant and one of the most dangerous. We even lost a family member. When this news broke, I was not even able to celebrate it with my family. We actually did it on a zoom call. In the midst of the pain, the anguish, the sadness, and the recovery, I was elevated to the highest office in the country. This just reminded me of how great my God is and everything that I have and that I am I owe to my Lord and Saviour Jesus Christ.

One of the biggest influences in my life and which I attain my success too is my spiritual life. I believe in Christ Jesus, and I am confident that I can do all things through Christ who strengthens me. I am currently serving as a member of parliament in the Parliament of RSA, and I serve in the Home Affairs portfolio committee. It's a new environment and a different experience, but it is a much greater responsibility and can become challenging at times. I am also still serving as the Chairperson of the Bayview Flats Residents Association, a position I have held since 1999. Over the years I have received many accolades, awards, and nominations both national and international. I received the Community Hero award in Chatsworth in the year 2002.

I was the recipient of the LETSEMA 2004 Award by ViaAfrica; this was an award for volunteerism and social entrepreneurship. I was honoured for the work on human rights through the organisation I have established, the Bayview Flats Residents Association (an award initiated and mandated by President Thabo Mbeki).

I also received the Ammen Awards for Community Upliftment in 2018, the Men of Valour Award 2018. In 2019 I was conferred with the Men of Valour Visionary in KZN Award. In the same year I also received the Most Influential Men of the Year 2019. During the lockdown in South Africa and the Covid pandemic, I was nominated on NEWS 24 as an Every Day Hero 2020 and was referred to as an Every Day Mandela. It was the greatest achievement to be contacted by Dr. Carl Wilson and to be awarded as on the Black Blazer Recipients. I was nominated by Shamilla Ramjawan for the Black Blazer of Excellence and Achievement Global 2021-2022. I later also received the Gold Men's Award for Leadership, Excellence, and Achievement. This was most humbling, and I will always be grateful to Dr. Carl Wilson for this acknowledgement.

I was also conferred with an Honorary Doctorate in Humanitarianism by the Global International Alliance and awarded with a Global Humanitarian Award; for this I must express my gratitude to Ambassador Lenora Wimberley-Peterson. None of these accolades and awards I take for myself or to become proud, but I dedicate it to the 23 years of community service and always give this back to my community in Bayview. They are the real reason for my acknowledgments. Had I not started my work in this community, the world would have never known about Brandon Pillay.

My most recent academic completion is a Masters in Administration (MAdmin), Public Administration from the University of Kwa-Zulu Natal (UKZN).

Nelson Mandela famously wrote about never stopping, always wanting, and needing to climb one more mountain. In my journey to finish my master's degree, I often drew on this for inspiration for the road I have travelled is an unusual one. I never went to university full-time but had to go through the Workers College while working full-time, defending and advancing the rights of my community and seeing to family matters. But once I was in a university environment, I knew that this is a world that would open new ways of looking at the world. And so, I moved through the gears as they would say, digging deep to pass the undergraduate years and then facing the daunting task of a MA. I was determined in the MA to produce research that would enable me to think through the vexed question of service delivery. There were times when I wanted to stop climbing as the path ahead was full of obstacles. Once more I drew on Mandela's words but also on had the support of my comrades, family, and most importantly my community.

I hope that this journey will inspire others. I have not stopped climbing. I have successfully enrolled at the University of Kwa-Zulu Natal and have received a full acceptance to commence with my PhD. I start my final academic journey in this month and hope to complete it in two years. As a doctoral student I will use my research to advocate for the betterment of services to communities. As I write these words, I cannot believe it. I know my parents in the heavens above will be smiling upon me. I know that Professor Fatima Meer would be immensely proud. The challenge, of course, is to turn our experience and our knowledge to the benefit of our communities. to be brave, to have the courage to stand up, to be able to learn, and to debate but not to impose. Above all always remember to humble yourself before God and the people you serve.

CYNTHIA SCHIAVETTO

Ken 'Dr. Smiley'
Rochon, Jr., PhD

The Evolution of Dr. Smiley

By Ken 'Dr. Smiley' Rochon, Jr., PhD

$36,000... that is what it would be worth to reach 10 million people. Do you want to reach 10 million people with your message? I do!

Most authors in a compilation book are never noticed or read. Why? Because there are too many chapters, and typically when you read one chapter, you may feel you have no reason or time to read more. This is connected to the value you received from the first chapter you selected.

If you select my chapter, this may be fortunate for you... as I intend to offer you $36,000 in value with no strings attached. Why? Because an author on a purpose driven life is not motivated by anything more than impact. So, if my chapter allows us to connect and share your story, then it will be a triumph and a compelling reason for writing this chapter.

When I was born over fifty years ago, I had no idea who 'Dr. Smiley' was, nor did I have any inclination he would be me.

I was born in Warwick, Rhode Island, and whisked away to Paris, France, as an Army brat. Twelve years and twelve countries later, I was back in Rhode Island trying to figure out how to use a phone. After devoting my life to soccer and believing this would be my life, I was depressed and disappointed that the return to America would be void of my biggest passion... Soccer. Pele was my role model, and he could not prepare me for the life I would lead in a small farm town in Galesburg, Illinois. This town was so isolated, that I was accused of being a 'Nazi Nigger Lover' because I came from Germany and was unaware that discrimination was a way of life in this town. The school was integrated, but the real estate told a different story. If you were on this side of the tracks, you were white, and the other side was predominantly black.

The reason I share this part of my life was that my dad and mom never taught me about discrimination or that it even existed. My mom was a fan of the American Indian and made it clear that the 'White Man' was the culprit of fairness and freedom. Her last thoughts as a victim of Alzheimer's were to support the American Indian and expose the atrocities of the White Man on this beautiful culture and race. Mind you, my mom is white, married to a white man.

I always wanted to be an author and more importantly matter in the world. I defined being an author as someone who was credible and worthy of attention and merit. Over thirty years of believing this never caused me to even write one sentence in a book... until I was a caregiver for my mom. That was the catalyst to stepping into my power---one born of fear I would die before I ever did anything to make a difference. I am not sure if all humans feel this way, but I certainly knew I could not be a person without a book.

This ignited action and a book thirteen months after my mom passed... titled 'Becoming the Perfect Networker... Succeeding I Connection @ a Time'.

This was a financial disaster, and any sane person would have written off the $22,000 loss as an act of ignorance. But a prayer to God helped me understand this was a message that most authors experience---perhaps a smaller financial loss, perhaps larger. Most quit with this impossible challenge to get a return on the investment (save the return on the effort). I would have quit, too, but God was clear... this was a lesson on how messed up self-publishing could be for a new author.

God and my mom were teaching me my most valuable lesson... a

Legacy is earned with an unstoppable attitude. I invested another $3000 to republish and reprint this grammatically incorrect nightmare. It was grammatically incorrect because of hiring a college professor in Florida that obviously did not have a clue about editing or writing. He fleeced me for over $1000, and a lesson was learned that without social proof, testimonials, and vetting, you are positioning yourself as a lamb ready to be fleeced or slaughtered of any dreams you will chase in the future.

Perfect Publishing was born because of this nightmare. My valuable lesson created a much needed company to protect future authors of bad decisions. I learned quickly how many leaders would love to do their book but just didn't understand how to complete it. I learned this firsthand by offering a $5000 'How to Write Your Book' program for FREE. Roughly ten people joined this program, and only one completed it. Why? Because it is confusing and overwhelming. How could I help more people step into their power to be an author, an inspiration, and a legacy for the people they loved? I needed to go back to the drawing board and find out where the pitfalls are that stop people.

The first pitfall was being inspired enough to even do the book / project. Many leaders just didn't know if they were worthy of being Authors. Many thought 'I need to accomplish more before I can write this book', or 'I need more money, success, or perfection in my life'. Not knowing the gifts, they had to share with the world already existed in their hearts and minds.

My focus became on how to overcome this challenge. I figured it out with some very simple out of the box techniques that caused almost 100% of my writers to become authors. It was about inspiration and breaking down the project into bite size weekly portions. Typically, a leader was able to complete this process in 3 to 6 months when I finally understood the dynamics of what would motivate them to compete, complete, and lunge into the finish line of being the new identity of an author.

The second issue became very clear to me that moving a book required a marketing approach and system---one fueled by social proof and testimonials. This was another gap that was causing authors great frustration. Most authors (almost 99%) were writing their first book, and the sales were so low that there just wasn't a desire to write another book. "Why would I write another book after I just wrote my best book… that took my life to create?" This was the question that was either internally plaguing them or that was shared with me with despair and disgust.

It was evident that there must be an approach or sequence that is causing this demise of the author's impact. It was quickly cleared up when I looked up their Amazon book listing and their social media. It was as if they believed that the book being delivered from their hearts and minds would magically awaken the world or through some osmosis would get into their avatars' being. I later termed this the Doctor Delivering the Baby (book) methodology. Basically, that when the book is printed, magically the world will find out about this birth.

As I have studied this insane perspective that the world is awaiting your book (unless you are an influencer with an enormous following), there is no one who knows your book exists… save the family you shared this dream with and your friends that will out of obligation buy your book for $20 with almost no intention of consuming, sharing, or being impacted by your brilliance. Because your friends know you, they have a difficult time adjusting to see you be bigger than how they define you in their lives.

This challenge is universal. Hence the reason when you make it big, your friends show up sharing they know you. ☺ Unless your friends have influence, I have learned it is best to show up as an unknown and create an identity you wish to be taken serious for being. I recently became 'Dr. Smiley'. This was welcomed in the new world. But it just could not be taken seriously by my family... well, my son loves the name and probably overstates my fame at this point. But having a young son to motivate you to be his hero is a gift in and of itself.

What I have learned is that I was almost 99% incorrect in how much proportion of my resources (money and time) should be spent on making my book versus moving my book. It turns out that if you spend three months or even one year writing your book, you are only doing what an Olympic athlete would do to get to the starting line of his/her performance or race. In other words, if you only wrote a book and thought that all the writing was the win, you would be thinking that all your workouts to qualify to be in the Olympics should be a medal earned. You have earned almost nothing by printing your book. I don't say this to be cruel or dissuade you from a wonderful accomplishment for your immediate family and friends. I am only putting this in perspective that there are over 7 billion people on this planet. What percentage are you impacting, inspiring, and causing to be fans of your passion and purpose?

My goal when I complete a book is never to stop marketing or printing it. That changes the book accomplishment to almost 1% of the work. I spend about 99% of my resources (money and time) making sure the book has impact. The closer I am able to be to 99%, the closer I have found the book impacts the world instead of only qualifying to compete to qualify to be at the Olympics. ☺

My final awakening of publishing is the misconception of moving a book versus creating abundance. A book is not just a delivery project to your family or even the world; it is hopefully a means of positioning you to be a solution, a leader, an expert, a sought-after sage of your domain. My book 'Becoming the Perfect Networker... Succeeding 1 Connection @ a Time' positioned me as 'The Man Who Wrote the Book on Networking'. I was on over 50 podcasts, and I became relevant to people who were just going to networking events and collecting cards. I became a prodigy of Bob Burg's 'Go-Giver' which inspired me to stop networking and start 'net-giving'. Instead of focusing on me, I moved to focus on who I could connect my network to create synergy, collaborations, joint ventures, and ultimately fans of my KEEP SMILING movement. The book broke several unofficial world records. It was the first book to have a ribbon on the front cover stating, 'Almost 100 Books Sold'. This little red ribbon was one of the biggest reasons I was selected to be on so many podcasts. They shared you are either very funny or crazy. Either way, it will make for a great show.

This book was also the first book to start on page '-1' and proceed to page '0' featuring the chapter 'The Defeatist Attitude' in order to make the point we must shift from believing we are not powerful to believing we create our happiness, our life, and our success. There were several other aspects that made this book a groundbreaking success in bringing business---humor (and color illustrations) together to provide the reader with page turning engagement and smiles.

My interests turned to publishing and writing books that didn't seem to exist on searches I did for children's books, linguistics, travel, etc. An eight-year dive into a project titled 'Making Friends Around the World' would be the first 'Decalingual' book in history.

In 2015, I met a man whom I lovingly refer to as a 'Prophet of Joy'. His name is Barry Shore. He simply handed me a card with

'KEEP SMILING' as the two words that would awaken my soul much like John Belushi in the movie 'The Blues Brothers' where he 'Sees the Light' and does cartwheels after experiencing James Brown and a concretion literally flipping and flying in the air with jubilation. I couldn't stop thinking about how congruent this message was to my mom's ability to bring positivity to my life, my family, her students, and her friends.

I shared with Barry that this card had awakened my soul, and I believe after his responses to what he is doing with the card, that I could create a movement. Little did he know that day that the card would be photographed thousands of times with amazing authors, business entrepreneurs, leaders, models, musicians, speakers, and anyone sporting a beautiful smile (teeth or not).

With all these photos taken, it was an easy decision to see what would happen if I created and published a little 6 x 6 book with all these amazing smiles and choose one of the leaders to share their story. We have almost 200 of these thematic books on Amazon and on our website (www.theKEEPSMILINGmovement. com) for FREE. Special thanks to our executive director, Dr. Andrea Adams, for her tireless commitment to keeping the movement … moving. She put on the map a legitimate 501c nonprofit with a mission of helping save lives with dental and mental wellness. The book 'The Science of Smiles' was released to share the importance of Smiles as part of your daily nutrition for your soul.

After completing my 36th book 'The Amazon 5 Star Review Club' book, I feel I have unleashed possibly my best work. It is a free book I provide to help authors get access to amazing content and return their appreciation in the form of a review on Amazon. This is the ultimate thank you to authors who have basically shared their souls for the sole purpose of impacting your life.

I've found my best strategy for making a difference in the world… is keep writing and keep giving my books away to people who need a solution to something I have written about. I average giving over 1 thousand books away a year (pre-pandemic) and over 10 thousand books a year as eBooks. If your book inspires someone to be better or awakens them to focus on you as a solution to their happiness, I assure you life will be better for both of you.

My favorite year of my life is ironically 2020---not because of the pandemic, of course, but because of what the pandemic caused, created, and inspired… a renaissance in my life and my son. Before the pandemic, my son (Kenny Rochon, III, aka K3) was not an author. He now has 6 books and aims on having 10 by his tenth birthday. His first book was simply a joke book that was in essence a compilation of jokes we found on Google that made him laugh. This book put him on the map because of the strategy I created around his book. He currently has over 150 five-star reviews for all his books because he understands at age 8 how to convert sales into testimonials and reinvest his profits proportionally into future books.

It was also the year I started my dissertation through the International University of Entrepreunology with a PhD in Philosophy. This gave rise to a new way of being identified… 'Dr. Smiley'. I come from a family of high learners, so this was a prestigious advance on my degrees, but my true motivations were to make my mom proud, and for my son to see when the chips are down, you can still come out on top if you want this enough.

My biggest legacy triumph is and probably will be my son's renaissance into authorship during this year of uncertainty. To my son, the pandemic was an opportunity to be home and not have to go to school. He didn't know what hit him when I shared,

I would be teaching him what he was missing... if he was in college. He questioned me several times asking me if I was sure a second grader should know the military alphabet, countries, and flags of the world, the periodic table, and sign language. I responded, 'Only if you are going to be a future leader'. He bought it, and we worked on his grasp of knowing the above with competency that would impress any adult. We soon discussed the possibility of him being an author before his 7th birthday. He was open to this as it was a book entitled 'Kenny's Favorite Jokes'. He even had a page with some of his originals which will remain my favorite forever.

When the book was delivered to him on his birthday (June 14th / 'Flag Day'), he was concerned with only one thing... is it on Amazon and could I prove it. The delivery of this beautiful color book created only about 1% of the excitement he expressed when he did indeed see his book and name on Amazon.com. This was one of my proudest moments as a father.

He has since arranged, googled, searched, and put together 'Kenny's Favorite Riddles', 'Kenny's Favorite Science Facts', 'Kenny's Favorite Things to Know' and 'Kenny's Favorite Trivia'. He is finally paying tribute to his birthday theme of patriotism with his newest book 'Kenny's Favorite Places in America' with shoutouts to his favorite restaurant 'Mission BBQ' that he hopes will show off his books at all 150 restaurants.

Future projects are 'Kenny's Favorite Phobias to Conquer' which will help children and maybe even adults overcome fears that are only in their head.

The reason I chose to invest in being a contributor of this wonderful book is because I believe in a publisher bringing together amazing leaders and creating a collaboration of heart centered thought leaders who together bring more focus to this project because they work together to share it matters.

To return to my opening sentence... '$36,000... that is what it would be worth to reach 10 million people. Do you want to reach 10 million people with your message?' I do. This is my mark and largest project of my life thus far. I intend to honor great inspiring leaders with a 'Chicken Soup meets TED Talk' formula for inspiring HOPE in the world. The project is titled 'D.O.S.E. of HOPE' and the acronym stands for the amazing chemicals God has created that are released when we feel alive and have 'HOPE' (Dopamine, Oxytocin, Serotonin, and Endorphins).

Just as Simon Sinek identified the importance of a company knowing the 'Why' and how to create a culture that attracts consumers who relate and become ambassadors of your brand, I decided to research the impact of asking the question 'Who Am I?' and 'How did I create my Who?'. Turns out the more we commit, devote, and invest (as referenced in Malcolm Gladwell's book 'Outliers'), the more we will create a 'Who' we love. This relationship to our love of ourselves allows us to create an equally powerful 'Why' otherwise known as a 'Purpose'. The higher the variable of 'Purpose' we claim as it relates to the needs of humanity, the higher our 'How' will be (also known as your 'Impact' in the world).

So the variables can be shown as:

$$Y \times W \times H = Sph$$

('Y' = You; 'W' = Why / Purpose; 'H' = How / Impact and 'Sph' = Smiles per Hour)

This is a TED talk in the making that I believe will even impress Simon Sinek. But I am most hopeful that it becomes a new way of looking how to shift our focus from things that will never make us happy to our happiness being derived from our ability to bring happiness to others and the world. The close second ingredient

I work tirelessly to teach my son is the gratitude reflection time needed for us to have the capacity to understand that our power to impact the world is fueled by our gratitude for being alive.

A friend recently gave me a wonderful acronym for H.O.P.E. ... 'Hold On Pain Ends'. This inspired a book to honor my mentor Barry Shore, aka 'The Ambassador of Joy' and my co-founder of the KEEP SMILING movement to publish our first book together... 'A Pocket Full of Acronyms'.

A venture called 'Amplifluence.com' is being launched as a tour around the world to help leaders have more impact with their message and mission in life. Michelle Mras, founder of the 'Hold My Crown' series, and Todd Westra are co-founders of something I believe will harness all the energy put into the KEEP SMILING movement and PerfectPublishing and create an impressive marketing system that helps authors be better speakers and speakers become (better) authors using funnels, monetization strategies designed to fuel their careers and dreams.

Every book I have mentioned in this chapter and the other 33 or so are all available for FREE because I believe a book is a business card with a big message designed to create conversations, opportunities, and legacy. Simply Kennect with me, and any and all of the ebooks are available for the asking.

My mom had an expression 'Look for the Good in People and You Will Always Find It'. I thank my mom every day I am alive to know that the world has good people worth amplifying their goodness... which is on over 2 million 'KEEP SMILING' cards that have been distributed to people who give the biggest gift that shows their soul at the highest frequency... a SMILE ☺

Roman P. Mosqueda, Esq.

Living a Full Life

By Roman P. Mosqueda, Esq.

By prevailing standards, I have lived a full and exciting life with numerous successes and dismal failures that I will highlight below.

Academic Achievements:

I graduated valedictorian in elementary school at the Iloilo American Memorial School in 1956; valedictorian in high school at the University of the Philippines Iloilo College in 1960; lone Magna Cum Laude in 1964 at the Ateneo de Manila University, majoring in Economics; and Cum Laude at the University of the Philippines College of Law in 1968; Master of Laws in May 1979 and Doctor of the Science of Law in December 1979 at The University of Michigan Law School.

I was elected as President of the Student Council of the Ateneo de Manila College of Arts and Sciences in 1963, and after I graduated from there in 1964, I was featured on the front page of the Manila Times. I was also elected as President of the National Students League after being elected as University Councilor of the U.P. Student Council in 1965.

I was granted the DeWitt Scholarship for Master of Laws and a research grant for Doctor of the Science of Law by The University of Michigan Law School and graduated with a doctoral dissertation in products liability: a comparative study in record time. My doctoral dissertation consisting of 596 pages was published by the U.P. Law Center in 1982.

Professional Achievements:

After passing the Philippine bar in 1969, placing only 13th place, I worked as an associate of the Quisumbing Law Office in Quezon City as a litigation lawyer. In 1976, I became the youngest law partner of the Quisumbing, Caparas, Ilagan, Alcantara, and Mosqueda Law Firm. As the only bachelor law partner of the firm, I was assigned to handle family law cases. In 1977, I wrote and published my first book: Marriage and Its Dissolution Handbook of 800 plus pages, wherein I advocated no fault divorce in the Philippines, which to-date has not been passed by the Philippine Congress.

Before publishing my first book on family law, I wrote legal stories in the weekly Philippine Women's Magazine for about a year. My writing skills were developed which led to the authorship of two law books and thousands of legal articles. I wrote for the Asian Journal in Los Angeles for several years.

The main reason why I graduated in record time at The University of Michigan was because I got A's in my courses, and I could not stand the Ann Arbor winter. I also wanted to go back to my law partnership in Manila, but an offer from the Florrie Wertheimer Law Office in Wall Street, New York City, proved to be overwhelming. After I was admitted to the New York bar on motion in 1980, I did jury trials in admiralty law at the Wertheimer Law Office at the Southern District Federal Court in Downtown Manhattan.

After my summation in a jury trial, Federal District Judge Knapp of the Southern District of New York complimented me by saying on the record that: "That was the best summation of making something out of nothing I have ever heard!" The jury verdict went against me in a very difficult case to prove in 1981. I stayed in Wall Street for two years until in 1982. My wife and I moved to Los Angeles, where I have been a solo practitioner with some associates ever since.

I have been fortunate to receive multiple law practice awards through the years: Million Dollar Award Forum, Super Lawyer in Immigration Law for Southern California, 2014-2021, Trial

Master, Best Family Law Lawyer for many years, 10 Best Personal Injury Attorney for California, Elite Civil Litigation Advocate, and many more.

I have been a licensed real estate broker in New York and in California since 1991. My real estate law practice has been augmented by my broker's license. For a short time in the 1990's, I was a licensed insurance agent with Primerica. I have been a CA State Bar arbitrator for attorney fee dispute resolution with the LA County Bar Association and a pro bono legal counsel of numerous Fil-Am associations in Southern California, such as the Ilonggo Association, Fil-Am Press Club, Guardian Angels Foundation, Fil-Am Kasama Foundation, and Philippine Medical Association.

Love and Family Life:

I had my share of girlfriends in the Philippines and New York before I met the most beautiful and intelligent lady doctor in New York in 1981. She graduated Cum Laude at the University of Santo Tomas College of Medicine in 1976 and was a resident in Internal Medicine at the St. Vincent Hospital in Manhattan, when I met her at a double date with my Ilonggo friend in New York, Tony Tiongco.

We dated several times, and after about seven months, I proposed. We got married in on June 6, 1982, at the Jesuit cathedral on Park Avenue, New York City. My best man was my brother-in-law, Dr. Jose Maria Porquez, a surgeon in Monroe, Georgia, and Mariedel's bridesmaid was her Korean friend, Yongco. My nephews and nieces (children of my sister Linda) were ring bearers and flower girls.

After my wife Mariedel Leviste finished her residency in New York, we decided to move to California in 1982. She liked Sausalito up north, but I had to study for the California bar exams in Los Angeles, staying at my auntie Maggie's house. I was offered an associate job by Baker & McKenzie in San Francisco, but my wife was already working in Los Angeles. So, we decided to put up my own law office and practice in Southern California. I passed the California bar on first take in 1984. We have a pretty daughter, Kristine, who was a finalist in Miss Philippines and graduated with a business degree at the Cal State Northridge. Our only son, Ryan, graduated in Philosophy at UCLA and then at the University of San Diego Law School on scholarship. He is presently assisting me at my law office during the pandemic. Both Kris and Ryan are still single. I do not have any "apostolic" mission so far.

Both actively in practice of our procession, my wife and I spend quality time with our two children. I have brought them to violin and tennis lessons in Los Angeles. Both played tennis for their schools. Ryan was the lead singer of a rock band before he attended law school. I took voice lessons while practicing law in Manila. My mother also had me take piano lessons. I also play the flute and clarinet. My main hobby is ballroom dancing. I have YouTube dance showcases with dance partners, April Bose, Noemi Hota, Crystal Chin, and Anne Montserrat and dancing the slow waltz, cha cha, Argentine tango, rumba, fox trot, and salsa. I also have at least three YouTube singing showcases: O Holy Night, Ave Maria, and Ako Ay Pilipino. My wife also showcased salsa and Egyptian belly dancing. She has her own dance instructor and partner. Our dance partners make us look good that we cannot do ourselves.

My claim to fame is the erection of my bronze bust at the Guimaras State College in Jordan for my donation of six hectares for the Mosqueda campus, earning me the unexpected reputation as a living legend. My singing, dancing, acrylic painting, and playing musical instruments have also tagged me as "Renaissance man," undeserved compliments by my Facebook friends.

My parents were both physicians and graduates of the University of Santo Tomas College of Medicine with my mother graduating Summa Cum Laude. My dad was a sought-after surgeon in Iloilo City who later was elected the first Vice-Governor of Iloilo Province. I sometimes wonder what if I took up medicine instead of law. I was a mama's boy. My mom was an OB-GYN who owned the Mosqueda Pharmacy, an enterprising member of the Palanca clan of twelve siblings from Victorias, Negros Occidental. I was born in Estancia, Iloilo, the hometown of my dad. I am a GI, Genuine Ilonggo "na malambing." (soft-spoken).

I would like to be remembered as generous, hardworking, excellent lawyer, and loving family man. Retirement is still far from my mind despite my advanced age. I keep my memberships in the Fourth Degree and color guard of the Knights of Columbus and Knights of Rizal in Los Angeles. I was Past President of the Wilmington and Historic Filipinotown Rotary Clubs and Chair of the Asian Pacific Centers for Counseling and Treatment for about fifteen years in Los Angeles County.

I consider myself blessed by the Almighty! Thank you, Carl Wilson, for my selection in the Black Blazer book as co-Author with others such as Chuck Norris and the nomination of Queen Corazon Ugalde Argenta of the Red Blazer book.

Fiat Dei Voluntas. (God's will be done.)
XXXX

Apostle Hezekiah Sherley III

Born to Lead

By Apostle Hezekiah Sherley III

My Name is Hezekiah Sherley III. I was born June 24, 1972, in Indio, CA. I officially moved to Clovis, New Mexico, from San Diego, CA, in 1987, where I currently reside. After being a member of the Bethlehem Baptist Church for some time, GOD called me to his Kingdom on Sept 19, 1991. After about a year I began to seek GOD for my purpose. In 1996 GOD called me to The First Church of God in Christ under The Bishop W.C., and Lady Ange Green, where I was called to the ministry in 2000. I then was ordained under the direction of Pastor David Dawson of Pure Heart Word Center in 2002. After 5 years of 5 a.m. prayer, GOD commissioned me to the call of pastor of the Agape Love Ministries, where I currently pastor today. Success to me is knowing and doing the will of GOD. I feel as long as this is done, you can and will not fail. I believe that following your dreams as well as your heart will forever make you happy.

The Spirit of The Lord said, "Go get my Covenant". The Holy Spirit dealt with me for hours; all I could do was weep. I had been leading 5 a.m. prayer with a remnant of intercessors for 5 years and heard prophecies that God was going to raise up a leader from among us. At the time I did not realize He was raising me up. See I was in a place where the majority of my family lived, and I knew everybody. I wanted to live in a big city and really had no desire to be in Clovis, NM Pastoring. I think because I was born in beautiful California, my desire was always to be in the big city.

The message I want to give to other young men out there is to be true to yourself. Allow the Lord to lead you. I have gone through ups and downs in my life, but I know that only God could allow me to make it through it all. I have faith in God because I know Him personally and not just from what I heard but from what I have experienced as a child of God. It is in Jesus that I have my very existence. My prayer for anyone that might read this book is that you get a personal relationship with Jesus Christ before it is everlasting too late. Choose on this day whom you shall serve as the word of God says.

I want to share a story that really blessed me with you. This is a very important story.

GET OFF THE NAIL

> There was a young man walking down the street and happened to see an old man sitting on his porch. Next to the old man was his dog, who was whining and whimpering. The young man asked the old man "What's wrong with your dog?"
>
> The old man said, "He's lying on a nail."
>
> The young man asked, "Lying on a nail? Well, why doesn't he get up?"
>
> The old man then replied, "It's not hurting bad enough."

Source | Les Brown, *Live Your Dreams*
(William Morrow Paperbacks, July 1994) page 194

I am grateful to God for my parents that instilled in me to allow the Lord to use me for His Glory. I love to sing and worship Him because I watched my mother give her gift of singing back to Him. Both of my parents have crossed over; it is not always easy to be in this earth realm without them. However, I know they are in a better place. I say to anyone that might read this book if your parents are alive and you have problems with them, fix them and love on them while you can because tomorrow is not promised.

Father God, I ask You to touch every individual all around the world that will read this global book. I ask that You open their spiritual eyes to allow them to see You and their spiritual ears that they may hear You clearly. I ask that You reveal Yourself to them like only You can. In Jesus Name I pray Amen.

Apostle Hezekiah Sherley Pastor & Founder of Agape Love Ministries and Yahwe International Church.

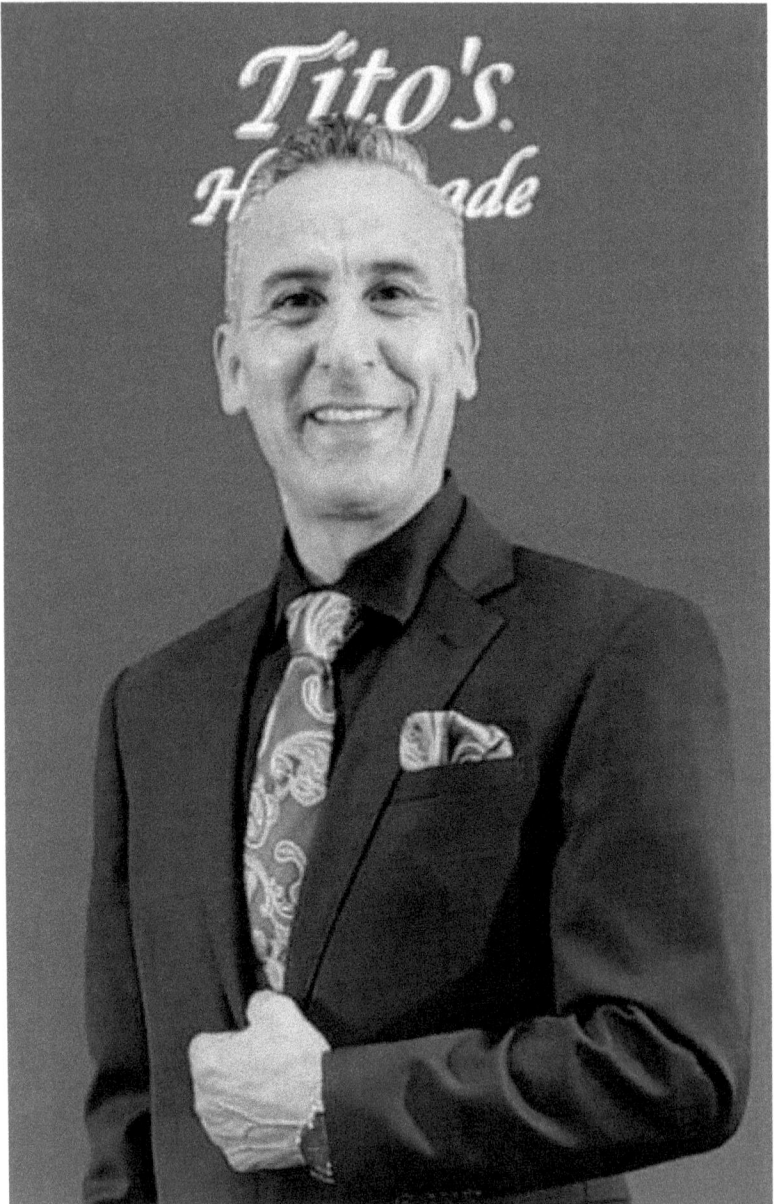

Pedro Frias

Positive Role Model

By Pedro Frias

My name is Pedro Frias Alvarez I was born June 29, 1969, in Guadalajara Jalisco, Mexico. My parents brought my four siblings and me to the U.S. when I was 5 years old; we lived in West Los Angeles. My parents were hard-working, honest people working full time jobs trying to survive and living day by day. My father worked at a clothes factory and was also a handyman that took weekend jobs; my brother Raul and I would help him on weekends doing yard work, tree trimming, roofing, tile work, and all types of work.

At the age of 12-13 years old my brother and I in the summer vacations would wake up early 5-6 in the morning to go bike riding and pick up aluminum cans that we found on the streets and help the lunch truck owners clean their trucks to make some money to buy our clothes we wanted or things we needed and also to help our parents. Our parents raised us to be responsible, honest, and hard-working and to contribute to the household needs and expenses at an early age. Lots of times when we went bike riding or to work, we would find bicycle parts and sometimes bicycle frames; we started to put bicycles together. Mr. Price, the landlord of the apartments where we lived, saw us working at an early age and let us use a room to store the bicycles and would then buy them from us when completed. I know he didn't really buy them to make a profit but to motivate us and do us the favor.

When I was young, I really liked school, but at the age of 13-14 we had new neighbors, and I became really good friends with their son. He was 3 or 4 years older than I was and was in a gang. We got along well, and I started to spend lots of time with my new friend and his friends staying up late hours of the night and started dressing like them and doing things I just did not do before he came along. My father after about a year or so of seeing what was happening decided to go on vacation to Guadalajara, Mexico, with the plan of moving back to our hometown. After about a month my mother received a call from my father letting her know to sell everything, and we moved back to Mexico. I was 15 years old, and we didn't understand what was going on at the time and were upset at the fact that we moved back to Mexico. We didn't know any of our relatives and had no idea of what school was like down there. My father told us when we arrived that we had two choices---to go to school or work. I decided to work and started working with my father selling all the lubricants for vehicles in the automotive locations in the little towns.

My father was an excellent salesman, and that's when I started learning about sales. I worked with my father for about 3-4 months but had a hard time working with him, so I decided to move to another state to work for my cousins doing the same thing. It was fun. I got to see different states in Mexico when we delivered the product, but I was only there about 6 months. I moved back to Guadalajara and started working for a gentleman recycling waste motor oil picking it up from mechanic shops and selling it to recycling centers. I made $15 pesos a week which was not enough to buy a pair of jeans, so after about 5-6 months of working with him 5-6 days a week 12 plus hours a day, I asked my boss for a raise and was denied. I gave my week's notice and borrowed my father truck and started my first business recycling motor oil and business going from making $15 pesos a week to making $100 pesos a day. That was my first business.

On November 1986 at the age of seventeen, I decided to move back to the U.S. due to differences with my father. I bought my bus ticket to Tijuana, and with only forty dollars in my pocket and two pairs of clothes headed back to the U.S., I arrived at my aunt Julia's house in Lynwood, California. I started looking for work but had no luck. A week later my Uncle Cosme went to pick me up and took me to his home in Pomona, California, and finally after about two months I found a job sanding furniture. About a week later my cousin's boyfriend Hector got me an interview at Seagate Substrates in Brea, California. On our way to the interview, Hector and I were in a car accident and arrived about three hours late. I had my interview and was hired on the night shift. I figured I would work both jobs because I needed the money to send some to my mother and had dreams that I wanted to make a reality. I was not able to work both jobs because the distance from one to the other and I would be late to the furniture place about half hour and the impossible.

My mother and older siblings focused on our goals and bought our first home in 1989 a year, and ten months after we were all back together in the U.S. I consider myself very fortunate that very positive people have been part of my life, and I always try to do the same for the people around me.

In 1996 I got married and was promoted to supervisor and was doing well financially, had a full-time job, and was also buying cars and products at auctions and making extra money. In 1998 I had a good relationship with my boss and good friend Joel McClure. In March 1998 we started a business. We started to do our research on different businesses and our finances and decided to open test only smog shop. It was a new program, and it went amazingly well and started making profits the first month. We opened two more test only stations in nearby cities within a year. Business was great, and we had employees running the smog shops, so we decided to open our first automotive 4X4 retail store and a second retail store within the same year also in 1999.

My wife Ana Frias and I bought our own home to start a family in 1998. In 2003 we bought a commercial property to build our building and move the automotive businesses there. In June 2005

I started doing mortgage and real estate in 2006, went thru the process, and became a real estate realtor. We sold two of the smog shops and closed one of the retail stores due to the retail business making minimum wages four dollars and cents as an operator. I was working long hours and any day I was asked to work, and shortly after I was promoted to waste water impossible.

In 2007 we started flipping houses; we started by buying one house at a time. After our fourth flip we picked up investors to buy homes at the county steps. We flipped over 20 properties from 2007- 2010 but had to shut down our last 4X4 automotive retail shop in 2008 to focus on flipping homes. In November 2010 real estate sales slowed down and decided to stop flipping homes and returned the investors back their money and (18%) profits.

One of our investor's parents' partners wanted to sell his agriculture farm, so we decided to buy it not knowing anything about farming but knew it was a must buy. The farm was already producing products, had buyers, and was making profits. We have picked up new clients for the farm. One of our products sells in all the U.S., and two of our other products sell worldwide. The agriculture farming continues to be a profitable business.

In 2018 I met Amelia Johnson, Esbeidi Crumbaker, and a group of goodhearted people that inspire others and are always there to help others. I'm grateful to be part of the many charity events that I have attended with them in addition to my wife Ana Frias and my in-law's family tradition for the last 20 years to feed the elderly.

2021 was a hard but exciting year. I had surgery in Guadalajara, Mexico, but with a positive and adventurous attitude my wife and I decided to buy a home in Colima, Mexico. I also started a business with Esbeidi Crumbaker in Tijuana, Mexico, a retail/

wholesale store; our goal is to have retail/wholesale stores throughout all of Mexico.

Seagate Substrates shut its doors in December 2000, and I have been self-employed for the last 21 years. I have owned nine different businesses and have decided to sell some of them; some have been closed down, and some continue running. We need to know when to make the decision to move on and focus on the ones that deserve to continue. I'm a firm believer that if you set your goals, you can achieve them. It takes long hours, hard work, and commitment. Always give 100% of yourself in everything you do, never be afraid to try again if it fails, always be positive and have positive people around you, and never be too proud to ask for help when you need it.

THE BLACK BLAZER

MEN ENTREPRENEURS "BLAZING TO SUCCESS"

Acknowledgements

I, Dr. Carl D. Wilson, Jr. want to take time to acknowledge all the co-authors of this book who shared their stories, anecdotes and advise to inspire you, the reader.

Forever grateful to: Asgar Mahomed, Saf Buxby, MJ Tolan, Kenrick McDonald, Jonathan Tarrant, Rodrick Chambers, Joseph Boy, Darryl Horton, Terrance Leftridge, Dr. Hassan Younes, David Adams, Tommy Willis, Spencer Muldrow, Mikey Adam Cohen, Brandon Pillay, Ken Rochon, Roman Mosqueda, Apostle Hezekiah Shirley, and Pedro Frias.

In addition, I want to acknowledge the publisher Angela Covany, the editor Dr. Randi D. Ward, and the formatter Marcy Decato for putting together a phenomenal book about men blazing to success.

THE BLACK BLAZER

MEN ENTREPRENEURS "BLAZING TO SUCCESS"

www.ingramcontent.com/pod-product-compliance
Lightning Source LLC
Chambersburg PA
CBHW062134020426
42335CB00013B/1211